THE GOOD ENERGY COOKBOOK

Lose Weight with 100 Recipes Inspired by Dr. Casey Means
to Boost Energy and Revitalize Metabolic Function

Sienna A. Wells

TABLE OF CONTENTS

Chapter 7: Energizing Lunches for Sustained Midday Vitality: Nutritious Recipes 43

Chapter 8: Dinners That Recharge and Heal: Nourishing Nighttime Recipes 54

Chapter 9: Plant-Based and Vegan Meals Recipes 65

Chapter 10: Snacks and Beverages for Optimal Energy: Delicious Recipes 76

FREE SUPPLEMENTARY RESOURCES

Scan the QR code below and immediately download the two freebies that you can keep on hand at all times to best track your weight loss journey.

 Food List

 21-Day Meal Plan

SCAN THE QR CODE TO DOWNLOAD

COMPLEMENTARY RESOURCES

WHY YOUR SUPPORT MATTERS FOR THIS BOOK:

Creating this book has been an unexpectedly tough journey, more so than even the most complex coding sessions. For the first time, I've faced the daunting challenge of writer's block. While I understand the subject matter, translating it into clear, logical, and engaging writing is another matter altogether.

Moreover, my choice to bypass traditional publishers has led me to embrace the role of an 'independent author.' This path has had its hurdles, yet my commitment to helping others remains strong.

This is why your feedback on Amazon would be incredibly valuable. Your thoughts and opinions not only matter greatly to me, but they also play a crucial role in spreading the word about this book. Here's what I suggest:

1. **If you haven't done so already, scan the QR code at the beginning of the book to download the FREE** SUPPLEMENTARY RESOURCES.

2. **Scan the QR code below and quickly leave feedback on Amazon!**

The optimal approach? Consider making a brief video to share your impressions of the book! If that's a bit much, don't worry at all. Just leaving a feedback and including a few photos of the book would be fantastic too!

Note: There's no obligation whatsoever, but it would be immensely valued!

I'm thrilled to embark on this journey with you. Are you prepared to delve in?

Enjoy your reading!

INTRODUCTION

What if the hidden key to conquering conditions like anxiety, heart disease, and even cancer lies not in expensive treatments but in the very cells that power our existence? This question challenges the typical narrative around health and wellness, urging us to look deeper into a realm often overlooked—our metabolic health. Welcome to a journey that promises to redefine how you perceive your well-being, offering you the keys to unlock a future where vitality and health are within your control.

In today's fast-paced world, health crises such as obesity, diabetes, heart disease, and mental health disorders are rampant. Many of us find ourselves caught in a cycle of seeking quick fixes, relying on medications and short-term solutions without fully understanding the root causes of these debilitating conditions. However, what if I told you that the foundation of your health, the bedrock upon which everything else is built, begins at a cellular level? The concept of metabolic health offers a revolutionary perspective that holds the potential to transform your life profoundly.

Metabolic health refers to how efficiently your body generates and utilizes energy from the food you consume. It encompasses processes like insulin sensitivity, lipid metabolism, inflammation regulation, and mitochondrial function. Essentially, it's the engine that powers your entire system. When your metabolic health is optimized, your body functions seamlessly, preventing many common health issues. Conversely, when there are disruptions in this intricate balance, a cascade of problems can ensue.

Imagine a world where the root causes of debilitating health conditions are understood through a single lens—metabolic health. This book will guide you to unlock the mysteries of energy production at the cellular level. Understanding metabolic health empowers you to make informed choices that enhance not just your physical health but also your emotional and mental well-being. By comprehending how your body metabolizes nutrients, you can tailor your diet and lifestyle to support optimal function, thereby staving off chronic illnesses and improving your quality of life.

Think about the implications of having the knowledge and tools to take control of your health destiny. In a time when medical advancements abound, the simplicity and power of dietary choices and lifestyle modifications often go unnoticed. Yet, these elements hold the transformative power to alter your life in ways you may never have imagined. No longer do you need to feel at the mercy of genetic predispositions or environmental factors. Through mastering metabolic health, you can enhance your body's innate resilience and capacity for healing.

Whether you're battling significant health challenges or simply striving to maintain a balanced, healthy lifestyle amid a hectic professional schedule, this book is designed with you in mind. It's written for health-conscious adults eager to understand and improve their metabolic function, those facing specific health issues who seek preventive and recovery strategies, and busy professionals who desire quick, nutritious recipes to integrate healthier habits seamlessly into their daily routines.

Your journey towards better health starts here. Within these pages, you will find an in-depth exploration of the scientific principles underlying metabolic health. We will delve into essential biomarkers that provide insights into your body's metabolic state, helping you assess and manage potential health risks effectively. You'll discover how certain dietary principles can fuel your body optimally, ensuring that you harness the maximum nutritional benefits from every meal.

This book isn't just about theory; it's about practical application. A clear, actionable four-week plan awaits you, meticulously crafted to kickstart your transformation. Throughout this period, you'll be guided step by step, learning to monitor your metabolic function and implementing small yet impactful changes to your diet and lifestyle. The goal is to make these modifications sustainable, fitting effortlessly into your daily routine so that they become second nature over time.

As you progress, you'll learn to recognize the foods that boost your metabolic rate, improve insulin sensitivity, and reduce inflammation. You'll delve into the importance of physical activity and how to incorporate simple but effective exercises that complement and enhance your metabolic health. Additionally, the plan includes stress management techniques and sleep hygiene practices critical to maintaining a balanced metabolic state.

Consider the cumulative effects of each positive change: increased energy levels, improved mood, enhanced cognitive function, and a fortified immune system. These benefits are not mere promises but achievable outcomes grounded in scientific research and real-life success stories. You might begin to notice weight loss, clearer skin, reduced cravings, and heightened mental clarity, all of which contribute to a tangible improvement in your overall well-being.

The intention behind this book is not just to inform but to inspire and empower. It's about equipping you with knowledge and practical tools to reclaim authority over your health. Picture being able to take control of your health destiny, monitoring your metabolic function, and making informed choices that empower every aspect of your well-being. By adopting the practices outlined here, you can break free from the constraints of poor health, leading a vibrant, fulfilling life that radiates vitality from within.

In the pages that follow, you will discover the five biomarkers that can help you navigate your health risks, the dietary principles that genuinely fuel your body, and a clear, actionable plan to revitalize your life in just four weeks. This book serves as your comprehensive guide to understanding and enhancing your metabolic health, paving the way for a future where you thrive in every sense of the word. So, let's embark on this transformative journey together, unlocking the full potential of your metabolic health and shaping a healthier, happier you.

CHAPTER 1: UNPACKING ENERGY HEALTH

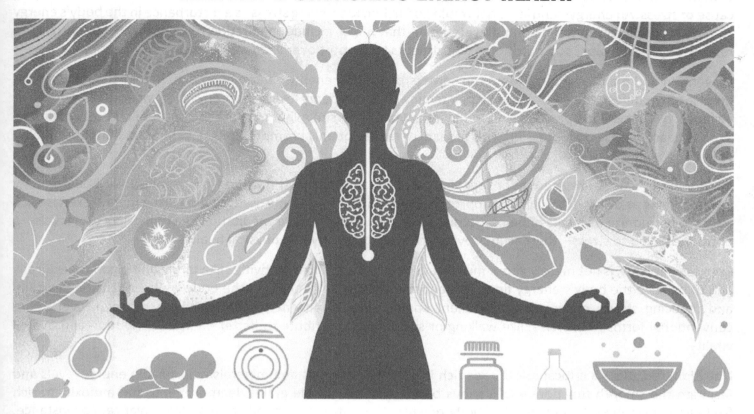

Unpacking energy health involves understanding how a unified approach to energy can profoundly impact overall well-being. Historically, health has often been addressed in fragmented ways, treating issues like high blood pressure, diabetes, or anxiety as independent problems without considering their interconnected nature. This method can be likened to repairing individual links in a chain while overlooking the chain's overall strength. In contrast, viewing health through an energy-centric lens offers a more holistic perspective, addressing the physical, mental, and emotional energies as an interdependent system.

In this chapter, we will delve into how maintaining optimal energy levels is crucial for preventing disease and promoting long-term health. We will explore the role of stress, poor nutrition, and lifestyle habits in depleting energy reserves and how these contribute to various health conditions. Additionally, we will discuss strategies such as integrating meditation, exercise, and balanced nutrition into daily routines to support a holistic energy-centric health model. By adopting these practices, individuals can enhance their quality of life, prevent chronic diseases, and maintain better control over their overall well-being.

FROM FRAGMENTED HEALTH TO A UNIFIED ENERGY APPROACH

Health has traditionally been seen as a series of isolated issues. The dominant medical model treats each problem—be it high blood pressure, diabetes, or anxiety—as a separate entity. This often leads to fragmented treatment plans where specialists address individual symptoms without acknowledging how they interplay within the whole body. This approach can be compared to addressing a single weak link in a chain while ignoring the overall strength and integrity of the chain itself.

In stark contrast, an energy-centric approach reimagines the body as an interconnected system. Here, physical, mental, and emotional energies are recognized as interdependent. Instead of focusing solely on alleviating symptoms, this perspective aims to balance these energies, fostering a state of holistic well-being.

Consider stress-related health issues as an example. Traditional medicine might treat stress-induced hypertension with medication. While effective in managing blood pressure, this method does little to address the underlying cause of stress. An energy-centric model would go further, identifying stress as a disturbance in the body's energy system. It would recommend a multifaceted plan that might include meditation to calm the mind, exercise to release physical tension, and nutritional adjustments to support overall energy levels.

Prevention and maintenance become the cornerstones in an energy-centric approach. Rather than waiting for diseases to manifest, the focus shifts to maintaining optimal energy levels to preemptively ward off ailments. For instance, by consistently practicing mindfulness or yoga, a person might mitigate the onset of chronic conditions such as heart disease or depression. This proactive stance not only promotes longevity but also enhances quality of life.

Integrating practices like meditation, regular exercise, and balanced nutrition can significantly boost energy levels, serving as pillars of this unified approach. Meditation, for example, is more than just a mental exercise; it's a tool to harmonize all facets of being. Studies have shown that regular meditation can reduce cortisol levels—a hormone linked to stress—thereby improving both mental clarity and physical health.

Exercise, similarly, is not merely about muscle building or weight loss. Activities like tai chi and qigong specifically aim to balance the body's energy flow. These forms of exercise strengthen the body while enhancing flexibility and reducing stress, making them excellent components of an energy-centric health regimen. Even more conventional forms of exercise, like walking or swimming, contribute to better energy distribution and overall vitality.

Nutrition, too, plays a critical role. Foods rich in essential vitamins and minerals help sustain energy levels and facilitate the smooth functioning of various bodily systems. Whole grains, lean proteins, and antioxidant-rich fruits and vegetables ensure that the body receives the nutrients it needs to maintain balance. For instance, Omega-3 fatty acids found in fish and flaxseed are known to support brain health and emotional well-being, which are crucial for maintaining a balanced energy state.

The benefits of adopting an energy-centric health model are manifold. Individuals often report heightened levels of energy and well-being. More importantly, they experience fewer instances of chronic illness and mental distress. Unlike traditional models that may lead to dependency on medications or therapies, energy-centric approaches empower individuals to take an active role in their health. By learning to manage their own energy systems through daily practices, people can maintain better control over their overall well-being.

In this context, it becomes essential to understand that the body, mind, and spirit are intrinsically linked. A disruption in one aspect can affect the others, creating imbalances that manifest as physical or mental illnesses. Thus, the energy-centric approach advocates for an integrated treatment plan that addresses all aspects of one's being. This holistic view not only treats diseases when they arise but also enhances preventive care, laying the groundwork for sustained health and vitality.

To better illustrate the shift from a traditional to a holistic model, consider a person suffering from chronic fatigue syndrome (CFS). Conventional treatments often involve a combination of rest, anti-inflammatory medications, and antidepressants. However, these treatments primarily target symptoms rather than the root cause. Meanwhile, an energy-centric approach would incorporate lifestyle modifications such as tai chi, acupuncture, and dietary changes to restore balance and improve energy flow. Research indicates that these interventions can alleviate symptoms more effectively by addressing imbalances at multiple levels.

Moreover, the holistic approach extends beyond the individual. Communities and healthcare systems that adopt energy-centric models often see improved public health outcomes. This is because these models encourage collective wellness practices and preventative measures, reducing the overall burden on healthcare resources. Initiatives such as community yoga classes, group meditation sessions, and educational workshops on proper nutrition foster a culture of well-being that benefits everyone.

Lastly, it's worth noting that adopting an energy-centric health approach is not about abandoning modern medicine. Instead, it's about integrating these age-old wisdoms with contemporary medical practices to offer a more comprehensive healthcare solution. Many practitioners advocate for a blended approach where

conventional treatments are used alongside energy-focused techniques to provide the best possible outcomes.

UNDERSTANDING ENERGY-CENTRIC HEALTH

Energy-centric health is a comprehensive approach that places the body's energy systems at the forefront of maintaining balance and vitality. This concept delves into the intricate networks like meridians and chakras, which are believed to play a central role in our overall well-being. Understanding these systems helps us appreciate how vital it is to keep our energy flowing smoothly.

Meridians, for instance, are pathways in the body through which vital energy, or qi, flows. These paths are crucial in traditional Chinese medicine (TCM), where they are used to diagnose and treat various ailments. When these energy channels are blocked or imbalanced, it can lead to physical or emotional issues. Similarly, chakras, originating from ancient Indian traditions, are considered centers of spiritual power in the human body. There are seven main chakras, each corresponding to different physical, emotional, and spiritual aspects of our lives. Maintaining their balance is believed to be key to sustaining health and preventing disease.

To support energy-centric health, several modalities have been developed aiming to correct any imbalances in the body's energy flow. Acupuncture, one of the most well-known practices, involves inserting thin needles into specific points on the body to stimulate qi flow through the meridians. This practice has been shown to help with pain relief, stress reduction, and even improving digestion and sleep quality.

Reiki, another popular modality, originated in Japan and involves a practitioner using their hands to channel energy into the patient's body, promoting relaxation, reducing stress, and facilitating healing. The belief is that by restoring energy balance, the body can better heal itself.

Biofeedback is yet another technique that bridges modern technology with ancient wisdom. It involves using electronic monitoring devices to help patients gain awareness and control over certain physiological functions, such as heart rate and muscle tension. By learning to regulate these functions, individuals can improve their energy flow and overall wellness.

Managing stress is crucial in energy-centric health. Chronic stress can wreak havoc on the body's energy systems, leading to blockages and imbalances that manifest as physical or emotional ailments. Techniques such as meditation, deep-breathing exercises, and yoga play a pivotal role in reducing stress. Meditation, for example, helps quiet the mind, allowing for a more harmonious flow of energy. Deep-breathing exercises enhance oxygen supply to the brain and muscles, promoting relaxation and stress relief. Yoga combines physical postures, breathing exercises, and meditation, providing a holistic way to reduce stress and maintain energy balance.

Nutritional choices are also fundamental in supporting energy-centric health principles. Foods that provide sustained energy, rather than quick spikes and crashes, are essential. Whole grains, such as oats and brown rice, release energy slowly, keeping you fueled throughout the day without dramatic highs and lows. Lean proteins, including chicken, fish, and plant-based options like beans and lentils, help repair tissues and maintain muscle mass, which is particularly important for energy production.

In addition to whole grains and lean proteins, incorporating a variety of vegetables, fruits, nuts, and seeds into your diet ensures a rich supply of vitamins and minerals necessary for maintaining optimal energy levels. For example, leafy greens like spinach and kale are packed with iron, which is crucial for oxygen transportation in the blood, thus boosting energy. Fruits like berries are high in antioxidants, which help combat oxidative stress and inflammation, contributing to better energy maintenance.

Hydration cannot be overlooked either. Dehydration can lead to fatigue and hinder both physical and mental performance. Drinking adequate water throughout the day supports cellular functions and keeps energy levels steady.

Another aspect to consider within energy-centric health is the alignment of lifestyle habits with natural rhythms. Practices like getting adequate sleep, engaging in regular physical activity, and spending time in nature can significantly influence the body's energy balance. Sleep, in particular, allows the body to repair and rejuvenate, while physical activity boosts circulation and energy flow. Time spent in nature has been shown to reduce stress and improve mood, further enhancing energy balance.

This multifaceted approach emphasizes that health is not just the absence of disease but a state of complete physical, mental, and emotional well-being. By focusing on maintaining balanced energy systems, we can prevent many common ailments and enhance our overall quality of life.

Moreover, educating oneself about these practices and being mindful of the body's signals can empower individuals to take proactive steps towards better health. Integrating energy-centric health practices into daily routines doesn't have to be daunting. Small, consistent changes can make a significant difference over time. For instance, starting the day with a few minutes of meditation, choosing a nutritious breakfast, and staying hydrated can set a positive tone for the day ahead.

HOW LOW ENERGY CONTRIBUTES TO DISEASE

In today's fast-paced world, maintaining high energy levels is paramount to overall health. However, when energy levels are consistently low, it can have detrimental effects on the body and mind, contributing significantly to disease development.

Chronic low energy is one of the primary culprits behind a weakened immune system. The body's natural defense mechanisms rely heavily on adequate energy reserves to function efficiently. When these reserves are depleted, the immune system struggles to combat infections and illnesses. This vulnerability can lead to frequent colds, flu, and other infections that further sap the body's energy, creating a vicious cycle that is hard to break. Ensuring ample energy supply is crucial for keeping the immune defenses robust and ready to tackle pathogens effectively.

Low energy levels don't just affect physical health; they also take a substantial toll on mental health. Conditions such as depression and anxiety are closely linked to chronic fatigue. Individuals experiencing low energy often find themselves trapped in a downward spiral where their mental health deteriorates, further draining their already scarce energy reserves. Depression, for instance, zaps motivation and makes even the simplest tasks feel insurmountable. Anxiety amplifies stress response, which consumes large amounts of energy. Addressing low energy is thus integral to breaking this cycle, improving both mental and physical well-being.

A significant factor contributing to chronic low energy is inadequate nutrition. Our bodies depend on essential nutrients to sustain cellular functions and overall vitality. When the diet lacks key components such as vitamins, minerals, and macronutrients, cellular processes become inefficient, resulting in diminished energy production. For example, insufficient iron intake can lead to anemia, characterized by persistent fatigue. Likewise, a deficiency in B vitamins can disrupt energy metabolism, leading to feelings of lethargy. Thus, a balanced diet rich in whole foods is foundational to maintaining optimal energy levels and preventing nutrient-related energy deficits.

To counteract low energy and its health implications, lifestyle changes play a pivotal role. Improved sleep hygiene is a cornerstone in this regard. Quality sleep allows the body to repair and recharge, making it essential for sustaining healthy energy levels. Establishing a regular sleep schedule, creating a restful environment, and limiting exposure to screens before bedtime are effective strategies to enhance sleep quality. Additionally, regular physical activity is critical. Exercise not only boosts physical stamina but also has profound benefits for mental health, releasing endorphins that enhance mood and energy.

Incorporating these lifestyle changes can significantly reduce the risk of developing chronic diseases. Physical activity promotes cardiovascular health, lowers blood pressure, and improves glucose metabolism, thereby preventing conditions like heart disease and diabetes. Furthermore, exercise can alleviate symptoms of depression and anxiety by promoting neurotransmitter balance and reducing inflammation. On the other hand, adequate sleep helps maintain hormonal balance, supports cognitive function, and reduces stress levels, all of which are vital for long-term health.

Making these adjustments might seem challenging, especially for busy professionals. However, integrating small, manageable steps can make a considerable difference. Prioritizing sleep hygiene might involve setting a consistent bedtime or creating a relaxing routine to wind down before bed. Incorporating physical activity could be as simple as taking short walks during lunch breaks or opting for stairs over elevators. These changes, though minor individually, accumulate to produce substantial improvements in energy levels and overall health.

Furthermore, understanding the role of nutrition can empower individuals to make better dietary choices. Planning meals that include a variety of fruits, vegetables, lean proteins, and whole grains ensures a steady supply of essential nutrients. Busy schedules often lead to reliance on convenience foods that are typically low in nutritional value. Preparing snacks like nuts, yogurt, or cut-up veggies can provide healthy, energy-boosting alternatives that keep energy levels stable throughout the day.

Addressing the multifaceted nature of low energy requires a holistic approach. While each aspect—immune function, mental health, nutrition, and lifestyle—plays a distinct role, they are interconnected and influence one another. Enhancing energy levels demands attention to all these areas simultaneously. By doing so, not only can individuals prevent the onset of chronic diseases, but they can also improve their quality of life significantly.

FINAL THOUGHTS

The chapter elucidates the imperative of viewing health through a unified energy lens, as opposed to the conventional fragmented approach. By recognizing and addressing the interconnectedness of physical, mental, and emotional energies, individuals can achieve holistic well-being. Practices such as meditation, regular exercise, and balanced nutrition are essential for maintaining optimal energy levels and preventing illnesses. These methods not only manage existing conditions but also act proactively to bolster overall health, highlighting the significance of an integrated treatment plan.

Moreover, understanding how low energy contributes to disease underscores the necessity of this unified energy model. Chronic low energy impacts immune function, mental health, and nutritional balance, creating a vicious cycle that exacerbates health problems. Lifestyle modifications, including improved sleep hygiene and regular physical activity, play critical roles in breaking this cycle. By integrating these practices into daily routines, individuals can significantly enhance their energy levels, reduce the risk of chronic diseases, and improve their quality of life. This holistic perspective empowers people to take active roles in their health, leading to sustained vitality and well-being.

CHAPTER 2: EMPOWERING YOURSELF THROUGH KNOWLEDGE

Empowering yourself through knowledge is a matter of harnessing information to make well-informed decisions about your health and well-being. In an era where data and advice are available in abundance, it becomes imperative to sift through these resources to find what truly benefits you. The ability to discern credible information from misinformation can significantly influence your health choices and overall quality of life. By questioning conventional wisdom and relying on evidence-based insights, you gain the confidence to trust your instincts over generalized advice. This chapter invites you to explore how critical thinking and informed decision-making can transform your approach to health.

Throughout this chapter, we will delve into various strategies to empower yourself through knowledge, starting with understanding the limitations of conventional wisdom and societal norms. You will learn the significance of evaluating diverse sources of information and consulting with healthcare professionals for personalized guidance. We will also discuss the impact of cognitive biases and societal pressures on health decisions, providing tools to counteract these influences. Furthermore, the principles of psychology and behavioral science will be introduced to help you form lasting, healthy habits. Finally, the chapter emphasizes the importance of emotional intelligence and mindfulness practices in making conscious health choices, encouraging you to build a supportive community that aligns with your well-being goals.

TAKE CONTROL: TRUST YOURSELF OVER CONVENTIONAL WISDOM

Understanding the importance of trusting your own instincts over societal norms or outdated advice is a crucial step in empowering yourself through knowledge. Our world is filled with an abundance of information, and much of it is presented as universal truths. However, it's essential to recognize that conventional wisdom is often based on generalized data, which may not suit individual needs.

Often, societal norms stem from historical contexts or traditional beliefs that don't necessarily apply to modern lifestyles or the unique circumstances of an individual's life. For example, dietary guidelines from decades ago emphasized high carbohydrate intake, which current research has shown may not be ideal for everyone, especially those dealing with insulin resistance or diabetes. By recognizing these discrepancies, you can begin to question whether such advice genuinely serves your health and well-being.

Taking control of your health requires making informed choices by researching and cross-referencing multiple sources of information. In today's digital age, a wealth of resources is available at your fingertips. Use reputable websites, scientific journals, and expert opinions to gather diverse perspectives on health-related issues. Consider consulting with healthcare professionals who can provide personalized assessments and recommendations based on your unique health profile.

It's crucial to differentiate between credible information and misinformation. Not all sources are reliable, and sensationalized headlines can often mislead you. Practice critical thinking by evaluating the evidence behind claims. Look for studies published in peer-reviewed journals and expert consensus rather than anecdotal evidence or unverified testimonials. Additionally, understand that science evolves; what might be considered accurate today could change with new research.

Empowering yourself through knowledge also involves understanding the basics of psychology and behavioral science to counteract societal pressures. Societal norms and expectations can significantly influence our behavior and decisions, often unconsciously. Social proof, for instance, is the psychological phenomenon where people mirror the actions of others, assuming they reflect the correct behavior. This can lead to following popular diet trends or wellness fads without considering their appropriateness for your specific situation.

By understanding these psychological factors, you can become more aware of how they impact your health choices. Educate yourself about common cognitive biases and heuristics that might lead you to make less-informed decisions. For example, confirmation bias causes individuals to favor information that confirms their pre-existing beliefs, which can prevent them from considering alternative viewpoints or new evidence.

Moreover, learning about the principles of motivation and habit formation can help you create lasting changes in your lifestyle. Behavioral science offers insights into how small, consistent actions can lead to significant improvements over time. Understanding techniques like goal setting, self-monitoring, and positive reinforcement can empower you to establish healthier habits despite external pressures.

It's also beneficial to explore the role of emotional intelligence in health decision-making. Emotional intelligence involves recognizing and managing your emotions and understanding the emotions of others. High emotional intelligence can help you better navigate social situations and resist peer pressure or societal expectations that don't align with your personal health goals.

Incorporating mindfulness practices into your daily routine can further reinforce your ability to trust your instincts. Mindfulness encourages you to stay present and attuned to your body's signals, enabling you to make conscious choices that support your well-being. Techniques like meditation, deep breathing, and mindful eating can enhance your self-awareness and decision-making processes.

Lastly, building a supportive community of like-minded individuals can bolster your confidence in trusting your instincts. Surround yourself with people who respect your choices and encourage you to prioritize your health. Engaging in discussions, sharing experiences, and learning from others' journeys can provide valuable insights and motivation.

LEARNING TO LISTEN TO YOUR BODY'S SIGNALS

Understanding and responding to your body's unique cues is a fundamental aspect of maintaining optimum health. Your body constantly sends out signals that indicate its current state of well-being or distress, and learning to interpret these signals can empower you to make better health-related decisions. By tuning into cues such as hunger, fatigue, and pain, you can gain insights into what your body needs and how it's functioning, which is crucial for both prevention and recovery.

Hunger is one of the most common signals your body uses to communicate its need for energy and nutrients. However, distinguishing between true hunger and cravings driven by emotional factors like stress or boredom can be challenging. True hunger usually builds gradually and is accompanied by physical signs such as stomach growling and low energy levels. On the other hand, cravings often strike suddenly and may be specific to certain unhealthy foods. Recognizing this difference can help you respond appropriately and avoid unnecessary eating, thereby supporting a healthier diet.

Fatigue is another significant signal that your body uses to convey various messages. Feeling tired can be a sign of inadequate rest, poor nutrition, or underlying health conditions. Chronic fatigue might indicate sleep disorders, nutrient deficiencies, or even more serious medical issues like thyroid problems or depression. Listening to your body when it tells you it's tired—and not just pushing through with caffeine or stimulants—can help you address the root cause and improve your overall well-being.

Pain, whether it's acute or chronic, is a clear indicator that something in your body needs attention. Acute pain is often a response to injury or immediate harm and generally subsides once the issue is resolved. Chronic pain, however, can persist for weeks or months and may be indicative of ongoing health problems like arthritis, nerve damage, or inflammatory conditions. Rather than ignoring pain or masking it with medication, understanding its source allows you to seek appropriate treatments and potentially prevent further damage.

To effectively track and interpret these bodily signals, consider keeping a health journal. Documenting your daily physical sensations, emotional states, dietary intake, and activity levels can reveal patterns that might otherwise go unnoticed. For example, noting when and what you eat can help identify triggers for digestive issues or food intolerances. Recording your sleep quality and energy levels can highlight connections between lifestyle habits and fatigue. This practice not only encourages mindfulness about your health but also provides valuable data that can be shared with healthcare providers for more informed consultations.

In addition to journaling, leveraging diagnostic tools can offer deeper insights into your body's signals. Blood tests, for instance, can detect nutritional deficiencies, hormonal imbalances, and markers of inflammation that might explain symptoms like fatigue or pain. Similarly, wearable technology like fitness trackers can monitor vital statistics such as heart rate, sleep patterns, and activity levels, providing real-time feedback on your health status. These tools can act as an early warning system, alerting you to potential issues before they become severe.

Developing personalized health strategies based on your body's feedback involves integrating the information you gather from these signals and tools into actionable steps. For instance, if you notice that you experience fatigue after consuming certain foods, you might explore dietary changes to see if avoiding those items improves your energy levels. If chronic pain is a concern, working with a physical therapist to develop targeted exercises and stretches could alleviate discomfort and enhance mobility.

Moreover, creating a balanced routine that addresses the core aspects of health—nutrition, physical activity, sleep, and stress management—is essential. Ensure that your diet is rich in whole foods that provide necessary vitamins and minerals, and stay hydrated. Incorporate regular physical activities that you enjoy, whether it's walking, swimming, yoga, or strength training, to keep your body active and resilient. Prioritize adequate sleep by establishing a consistent bedtime routine and optimizing your sleep environment. Finally, practice stress-reducing techniques such as mindfulness, meditation, or hobbies that bring you joy to maintain mental and emotional wellness.

Listening to your body's cues is not a one-time event but an ongoing process. As your life circumstances change, so will your body's needs and responses. Regularly reassess your health strategies and be open to adjusting them as required. This dynamic approach ensures that you remain attuned to your body's evolving signals and can proactively manage your health.

DECODING YOUR BODY'S DATA

Leverage medical tests and wearable technology to gain deeper insights into your health. Understanding your body's inner workings through data can empower you to make better decisions about your health and well-being.

Learning how to read and interpret common blood tests is a fundamental skill that can provide significant insights into your health. Blood tests like cholesterol panels, glucose levels, and hormone panels reveal crucial information about your metabolic function. For instance, cholesterol tests measure levels of HDL (good cholesterol), LDL (bad cholesterol), and triglycerides. High LDL and triglycerides can indicate an increased risk for heart disease, while high HDL can protect against it. Glucose levels are vital for diagnosing diabetes or prediabetes. Monitoring these levels helps you understand how your body processes sugar. Hormone panels, including thyroid, testosterone, and estrogen levels, can give insights into metabolic rate, energy levels, and overall hormonal balance.

Wearable technology, such as fitness trackers and smartwatches, has revolutionized how we monitor our health on a daily basis. These devices track vital statistics such as heart rate, sleep patterns, and activity levels. Heart rate variability (HRV) is one of the critical metrics measured by wearables. HRV indicates the variation in time between each heartbeat and can be a powerful marker of stress levels, cardiovascular health, and overall resilience. A higher HRV typically suggests a relaxed state, while a lower HRV might signal stress or fatigue.

Sleep trackers assess the quality of your sleep, identifying phases like deep sleep, REM sleep, and light sleep. Understanding your sleep patterns can help you make adjustments to improve sleep quality, which is pivotal for recovery and overall well-being.

Using this data to identify trends, potential health issues, and areas for improvement in your lifestyle is where the real empowerment begins. By regularly monitoring your blood test results and wearable data, you can detect patterns or anomalies before they develop into serious health problems. For example, tracking your glucose levels over time can help you see how different foods or activities affect your blood sugar. If you notice a trend of elevated glucose levels, you can take proactive steps by adjusting your diet or increasing physical activity. Similarly, if your cholesterol levels start creeping up, you might consider dietary changes, like reducing saturated fat intake or increasing fiber consumption.

The power of wearables extends to recognizing potential health issues early. Suppose your wearable device consistently shows low HRV or disturbed sleep patterns; these could be indicators of chronic stress or other underlying conditions. With this knowledge, you may pursue stress management techniques such as mindfulness, meditation, or even consult a healthcare professional for further evaluation.

Once you have gathered and understood your health data, leveraging this information to make informed choices is the next step. Personalized data enables you to create a tailored approach to improving your health. For instance, if your data reveals that your sleep quality improves with consistent bedtime routines, you might prioritize setting a fixed sleep schedule. Or, if your heart rate data shows positive responses to specific types of exercise, you could incorporate more of those workouts into your routine.

Furthermore, having concrete data allows you to set realistic and achievable health goals. If you're aiming to lose weight, regular monitoring of your glucose and activity levels can help you fine-tune your diet and exercise plans. If improving cardiovascular health is your goal, watching your HRV and cholesterol levels can guide you towards better dietary choices and effective workout regimens.

Integrating both medical tests and wearable technology into your health routine provides a comprehensive picture of your well-being. It's essential to remember that these tools are not a substitute for professional medical advice but rather a supplement that provides additional insights. Regular check-ups with healthcare providers ensure that you interpret and act on your data correctly. Combining professional advice with personal data empowers you to take a proactive role in managing your health.

To amplify the benefits, sharing this valuable information with your healthcare provider can lead to more personalized care. Equipped with detailed personal data, your doctor can offer more targeted recommendations that align with your unique health profile. This collaborative approach enhances the effectiveness of any interventions or treatments you may need.

SUMMARY AND REFLECTIONS

Empowering yourself with knowledge is essential for making informed health decisions. Throughout this chapter, we've explored how understanding the limitations of conventional wisdom and recognizing your unique needs can lead to better choices for your well-being. By questioning generalized advice and relying on credible sources, you gain the confidence to trust your instincts. This approach not only helps you navigate the vast amounts of information available but also empowers you to take control of your health journey.

Additionally, we've highlighted the importance of psychological awareness in making health decisions. Understanding cognitive biases and societal pressures allows you to resist trends that may not be beneficial for you. By integrating mindfulness and emotional intelligence into your daily life, you become more attuned to your body's signals and make choices that align with your personal health goals. Surrounding yourself with a supportive community further reinforces these positive changes, helping you maintain a proactive and informed approach to your well-being.

CHAPTER 3: PRINCIPLES AND PRACTICE OF ENERGY COOKING

Preparing meals that energize the body and mind involves understanding key principles and practical applications of energy cooking. This chapter delves into how whole, unprocessed foods serve as the foundation for a diet that sustains energy levels throughout the day. By preventing energy spikes and crashes through stable blood sugar levels, these natural foods offer long-lasting benefits. Additionally, the nutrient density of foods like leafy greens, berries, nuts, seeds, and legumes will be explored to demonstrate their role in providing essential micronutrients for efficient metabolic function and energy production. Balancing macronutrients—proteins, fats, and carbohydrates—is another crucial aspect covered in this chapter, highlighting how each contributes to bodily functions and energy maintenance.

Apart from nutritional content, the chapter also emphasizes the importance of hydration in managing energy levels. It discusses how water is involved in biochemical reactions that generate energy and offers tips on maintaining optimal hydration. Individual variability in dietary responses is another major theme, stressing the importance of tuning into personal signals to adjust food intake accordingly. Practical advice on incorporating small, manageable changes into daily routines, such as swapping processed snacks for whole food alternatives, is provided to help readers make gradual yet impactful improvements. Also included are strategies for mindful eating, portion control, and integrating nourishing ingredients into daily meal preparations for sustained energy and overall well-being.

FUNDAMENTAL PRINCIPLES FOR A VITALIZING DIET

Whole, unprocessed foods are the bedrock of an energizing diet. These foods retain their natural fiber, vitamins, and minerals, supporting sustained energy release throughout the day. Unlike processed foods—which often contain added sugars and unhealthy fats—whole foods contribute to stable blood sugar levels and prevent energy spikes and crashes. For example, choosing a piece of fruit over a sugary snack bar provides longer-lasting energy and essential nutrients without the empty calories. Incorporating items such as fruits, vegetables, whole grains, lean proteins, and nuts can significantly enhance your energy levels.

The role of nutrient density cannot be overstated in maintaining vitality. Nutrient-dense foods offer high levels of vitamins, minerals, and other beneficial compounds relative to their calorie content. This means you get more nutritional bang for your buck with every bite. Foods like leafy greens, berries, nuts, seeds, and legumes are examples of nutrient-dense options that provide essential micronutrients needed for efficient metabolic function and energy production. Consuming these foods regularly ensures your body has a steady supply of the building blocks necessary for optimal health and sustained energy.

Balancing macronutrients is another crucial factor in daily energy maintenance. Proteins, fats, and carbohydrates each play unique roles in supporting bodily functions and energy levels. Proteins are vital for muscle repair and growth, enzymes, and hormone production. Including sources like lean meats, fish, beans, and tofu in your diet can help meet your protein needs. Fats, particularly healthy fats found in avocados, nuts, seeds, and olive oil, are essential for cell structure, nerve function, and prolonged energy. Meanwhile, carbohydrates are the body's preferred energy source. Choosing complex carbohydrates such as whole grains, vegetables, and legumes over simple carbs helps maintain stable blood sugar levels and provides sustained energy release.

Hydration is another critical aspect of how we manage our energy levels throughout the day. Water is involved in virtually every biochemical reaction within the body, including those that generate energy. Even mild dehydration can impair cognitive function and physical performance, leading to fatigue and decreased productivity. Drinking adequate amounts of water helps maintain blood volume, supports nutrient transport, and assists in waste removal—all essential processes for keeping energy levels stable. Aim to consume at least eight glasses of water daily, adjusting for factors like physical activity and climate to ensure optimal hydration.

When discussing these principles, it's important to consider individual variability. Everyone's body reacts differently to dietary changes, so tuning into your own body's signals and adjusting as necessary is key. Some people may find they thrive on higher protein intake, while others might need more carbohydrates to feel energized. Paying attention to how different foods affect your energy levels can guide you in making personalized adjustments to your diet.

Implementing these principles doesn't have to be overwhelming. Start by making small, manageable changes such as swapping out processed snacks for whole food alternatives or incorporating more fruits and vegetables into your meals. Gradually increasing your intake of nutrient-dense foods will naturally crowd out less nutritious options without feeling restrictive. Additionally, balancing your plate with a mix of proteins, fats, and carbohydrates at each meal can help stabilize your energy throughout the day.

Considering hydration, make it a habit to drink water consistently rather than waiting until you're thirsty, as thirst can be a sign you're already dehydrated. Carrying a reusable water bottle with you as a reminder can help maintain regular hydration. Pay attention to signs of dehydration such as dark urine, dry skin, or frequent headaches, and increase your water intake if you experience any of them.

CREATING ENERGIZING MEALS WITH GOOD ENERGY PRINCIPLES

Crafting meals that boost energy is a key principle for ensuring both physical and mental wellness. By thoughtfully selecting ingredients and practicing mindful eating techniques, anyone can create a diet that supports sustained vitality throughout the day.

To begin with, incorporating a variety of colorful fruits and vegetables in every meal is essential. These natural sources of vitamins, minerals, and antioxidants not only enhance the meal visually but also contribute to overall energy levels. For example, adding bell peppers, spinach, and berries to various dishes provides an array of nutrients that support bodily functions and promote well-being. Aim to include at least three different colors on your plate, as this often correlates with a diverse intake of essential nutrients.

Mindful eating is another powerful technique to boost energy. This practice involves being fully present during meals, slowing down, and savoring each bite. When you eat mindfully, digestion improves and energy absorption is optimized. Take the time to chew food thoroughly; this aids in breaking down food particles more effectively, allowing digestive enzymes to work efficiently. Furthermore, by paying attention to hunger and satiety cues, you can avoid overeating and maintain steady energy levels throughout the day.

Balancing proteins, healthy fats, and complex carbohydrates is vital for creating energy-boosting meals. Proteins such as lean meats, beans, and legumes provide the building blocks for muscle repair and growth. Healthy fats like avocado, nuts, and olive oil are indispensable for brain function and hormone production. Complex carbohydrates found in whole grains, vegetables, and legumes release glucose slowly into the bloodstream, providing a sustained energy supply. A balanced meal might include a portion of grilled chicken for protein, quinoa for complex carbohydrates, and a salad dressed with olive oil for healthy fats.

Portion control is crucial for maintaining high energy levels. Consuming large quantities of food at once can overwhelm digestion and lead to sluggishness. Instead, aim for smaller, more frequent meals or snacks that keep your metabolism active. Listen to your body, and stop eating when you feel comfortably full. Overeating can lead to spikes in blood sugar levels followed by crashes, resulting in reduced energy and making you feel lethargic.

Lastly, integrating these principles into your daily routine need not be overwhelming. Simple tweaks to your current meal preparations can yield significant benefits. Start by planning your meals around fresh produce, whole grains, and lean proteins. Experiment with different herbs and spices to make dishes more exciting without resorting to processed ingredients.

RECIPES THAT EMBODY GOOD ENERGY PRINCIPLES

When it comes to starting your day with energy and vitality, breakfast plays a pivotal role. One of the most effective ways to ensure you fuel your body properly is by incorporating high-energy ingredients into your morning meal. A perfect example of this is a hearty bowl of overnight oats mixed with nuts and berries.

To prepare this recipe, begin by combining half a cup of rolled oats with half a cup of milk—dairy or plant-based, depending on your preference—in a jar. Add a tablespoon of chia seeds for an extra boost of fiber and omega-3 fatty acids. Stir in a handful of mixed berries, such as blueberries, strawberries, and raspberries, which are rich in antioxidants and vitamins. Top this mixture with a tablespoon of chopped nuts like almonds or walnuts for healthy fats and protein that will keep you feeling full longer. Seal the jar and refrigerate it overnight. By morning, the oats will have absorbed the liquid and softened, creating a nutritious and convenient breakfast.

For lunch, maintaining steady energy levels through balanced meals is essential. Consider a vibrant quinoa salad packed with lean proteins and leafy greens. Start by cooking half a cup of quinoa according to package instructions. Once cooked, let it cool and then transfer it to a large bowl. Add a generous handful of baby spinach or kale, which are excellent sources of iron and magnesium, crucial for energy production. Incorporate a serving of grilled chicken breast or chickpeas for lean protein. Toss in some diced bell peppers, cucumbers, and cherry tomatoes to add color and a variety of vitamins. For dressing, use a simple lemon vinaigrette made from fresh lemon juice, olive oil, salt, and pepper. This salad is not only refreshing but also provides sustained energy to carry you through the afternoon.

Dinner should focus on providing nourishment without being too heavy, helping you to wind down and prepare for rest. Opt for a meal featuring omega-3 rich fish, such as salmon, accompanied by roasted vegetables and brown rice. Begin by seasoning a salmon fillet with olive oil, salt, pepper, and a squeeze of lemon juice. Roast it in a preheated oven at 375°F for about 15-20 minutes until it flakes easily with a fork. While the fish is roasting, prepare an assortment of colorful vegetables like zucchini, bell peppers, and carrots. Toss them in olive oil, season with herbs like rosemary and thyme, and roast them alongside the salmon for about 25-30 minutes. As a side, cook one cup of brown rice according to package instructions. Brown rice is a great source of complex carbohydrates that provide lasting energy. Plate the salmon with the roasted vegetables on a bed of brown rice for a nutritious and satisfying evening meal.

Snacking can also be a valuable part of maintaining energy throughout the day, especially during late afternoons when you might need a quick pick-me-up. A nut-and-fruit mix combines natural sugars and proteins to deliver a quick energy boost. Create your mix by combining a variety of nuts such as almonds, cashews, and pistachios with dried fruits like raisins, cranberries, and apricots. Nuts provide healthy fats and proteins, while dried fruits offer natural sugars and fiber. This combination not only tastes good but also helps stabilize blood sugar levels, preventing energy crashes.

SUMMARY AND REFLECTIONS

This chapter has explored how essential principles like incorporating whole, unprocessed foods, nutrient-dense options, and balanced macronutrients can significantly impact your energy levels. By paying attention to hydration and being mindful of individual dietary needs, you can fine-tune your diet to maintain consistent energy throughout the day. Implementing these changes may seem daunting at first, but starting with small, manageable adjustments—such as replacing processed snacks with healthier alternatives and ensuring proper hydration—can make a big difference without feeling restrictive.

Crafting energizing meals is a practical way to harness these principles for both physical and mental well-being. Incorporate colorful fruits and vegetables, balance proteins, healthy fats, and complex carbohydrates, and practice portion control to create meals that boost vitality. Integrate simple and nutritious recipes into your routine to support sustained energy and overall health. By focusing on these foundational elements, you can develop a diet that not only fuels your body but also supports your long-term wellness goals.

CHAPTER 4: SYNCHRONIZING WITH NATURAL RHYTHMS

Synchronizing with natural rhythms involves attuning our daily habits to the inherent cycles within our bodies, particularly the circadian rhythm. Recognizing the importance of these natural processes can lead to enhanced well-being and improved health outcomes. Our bodies operate on a 24-hour cycle that influences everything from sleep and wakefulness to hormone release and digestion. When we align our activities with these rhythms, we optimize bodily functions and enhance overall vitality.

This chapter delves into practical strategies for aligning with natural rhythms to boost metabolic function and maintain energy levels. It covers how meal timing, physical activity scheduling, and environmental adjustments can harmonize with our internal clocks. Readers will find guidance on maintaining consistent meal patterns, selecting optimal times for exercise based on peak energy levels, and creating conducive environments for restful sleep. By adopting these practices, individuals can foster a balanced lifestyle that supports both physical and mental health.

HONORING YOUR CIRCADIAN RHYTHM

Synchronizing With Natural Rhythms for Improved Well-Being

Understanding and aligning with the natural rhythms of our bodies can significantly enhance our overall well-being. One of the most fundamental aspects of this is the circadian rhythm, a 24-hour cycle that regulates various bodily functions including sleep-wake cycles, hormone release, and other physiological processes.

The circadian rhythm acts like an internal clock, influencing when we feel alert or sleepy, when certain hormones are released, and how various bodily functions operate throughout the day. This rhythm is guided by external cues such as light and dark, meal times, and physical activity. When these cues are in sync with our natural rhythms, they help maintain a balanced and healthy lifestyle. Failure to align with these rhythms can lead to disruptions that affect our health and well-being.

One crucial area where synchronization with the body's internal clock can make a significant difference is digestion and metabolism. Eating meals at consistent times aligned with your circadian rhythm can improve digestion and nutrient absorption, leading to better overall metabolic function. For instance, eating breakfast around the time you naturally wake up prepares your digestive system for the day's activities and helps stabilize blood sugar levels. Ensuring that lunch and dinner occur at regular intervals supports ongoing metabolic processes and prevents the body from feeling undue stress caused by irregular eating patterns.

To guide you in aligning meal times with your body clock, consider keeping a regular schedule for your meals. Aim to eat breakfast within an hour of waking up. Make lunch the most substantial meal of the day between noon and 2 p.m., and finish dinner by 7 p.m. or 8 p.m. at the latest. This approach allows your body to efficiently process food and minimize late-night hunger, which can disrupt sleep and weight management.

Another significant aspect of synchronizing with natural rhythms involves planning physical activities based on your peak energy times. Most people experience a surge in energy and alertness mid-morning and early evening. Scheduling workouts or physically demanding tasks during these periods can enhance performance and efficiency. For example, if you typically feel more energetic around 10 a.m., this would be an ideal time for a challenging workout or an important meeting that requires sharp focus and quick thinking. Similarly, engaging in moderate physical activity in the early evening can help reduce stress accumulated during the day and improve sleep quality.

Conversely, there are periods when the body naturally dips into lower energy states, often post-lunch or late afternoon. These times are better suited for less demanding tasks or short breaks to rejuvenate before tackling the next set of activities. Recognizing and adapting to these natural peaks and troughs in energy can help you maximize productivity and maintain mental and physical stamina throughout the day.

Furthermore, disruptions in the circadian rhythm can have tangible adverse effects on health. Irregular sleep patterns, frequent night shifts, or extensive traveling across time zones can throw off the body's internal clock. This misalignment can lead to various health issues such as insomnia, obesity, cardiovascular diseases, and impaired cognitive function. Chronic disruption of natural rhythms places stress on the body, hampering its ability to perform essential functions smoothly.

For health-conscious adults seeking to enhance metabolic function, understanding the intricate role the circadian rhythm plays in regulating bodily functions is paramount. By aligning daily activities with natural rhythms, individuals can create an environment that promotes optimal health and well-being. Taking steps to regulate meal times, scheduling physical activities according to energy levels, and minimizing disruptions to the circadian rhythm can all contribute to a balanced and healthier lifestyle.

ALIGNING MEAL TIMES WITH YOUR BODY CLOCK FOR OPTIMAL ENERGY

Eating a balanced breakfast helps stabilize blood sugar and provide sustained energy throughout the day. A nutritious breakfast, often regarded as the most important meal, sets the tone for your body's metabolic processes. Starting the day with a combination of complex carbohydrates, protein, and healthy fats can prevent the mid-morning energy slump that many people experience. For instance, whole grain toast with avocado and eggs provides fiber, healthy fats, and protein, which together slow the release of glucose into the bloodstream. This results in steady energy levels and curbs hunger, preventing overeating later on.

Consuming larger meals earlier in the day aligns with natural digestive efficiencies. Our bodies are more efficient at digesting and metabolizing food during daylight hours. Eating your heaviest meal in the middle of the day when digestive enzymes are most active can enhance nutrient absorption and energy utilization. This practice supports liver function and overall metabolism. For example, having a substantial lunch that includes a variety of vegetables, lean proteins, and whole grains can keep you full and energetic throughout the afternoon, reducing the need for unhealthy snacks. Aligning our eating patterns with our body's natural circadian rhythms essentially optimizes digestion and maintains energy levels.

Skipping meals or erratic eating patterns can disrupt hormonal balance and lead to fatigue. When you miss meals or eat at irregular times, your body's insulin levels can become unstable. Insulin, a hormone that regulates blood sugar, plays a crucial role in how we feel throughout the day. An irregular eating schedule can cause spikes and drops in blood sugar, leading to feelings of lethargy, irritability, and brain fog. Over time, these fluctuations can also affect the production of hormones like cortisol, which manages stress responses. Skipping meals also prompts the body to store fat as a reserve, potentially leading to weight gain. Consistently eating at regular intervals helps maintain a stable internal environment, essential for energy and health.

Properly spaced meals prevent late-night eating, which can interfere with sleep quality and weight management. Eating late at night forces your body to work on digestion when it should be focusing on rest and recovery. This can disrupt sleep patterns and reduce the restorative quality of sleep, making you feel tired and less focused the next day. Late-night eating is often associated with poorer food choices and higher caloric intake, contributing to unwanted weight gain. Maintaining a routine of well-spaced meals throughout the day can help curb late-night hunger. For example, if you have an early dinner around 6 PM, you can wrap up your day without needing another heavy meal before bedtime. This ensures a good night's sleep and helps in managing weight.

RESTORING WHAT'S BEEN LOST

In today's fast-paced world, it is increasingly essential to incorporate healthy habits that align with our natural rhythms. One effective strategy is to integrate regular movement breaks into our daily routines, which can significantly counteract the sedentary nature of contemporary life. Many people find themselves sitting for extended periods due to desk jobs or prolonged screen time. This lack of movement contributes to various health issues, including reduced metabolism, back pain, and cardiovascular problems.

To combat this, consider setting a timer to remind yourself to stand up and move every hour. Even short activities like stretching, taking a brisk walk, or performing light exercises can make a world of difference. Studies have shown that breaking up long periods of sitting with brief bursts of activity can improve circulation, boost energy levels, and enhance overall well-being. Additionally, incorporating movement into your daily routine can help maintain a healthy weight, reduce stress, and increase productivity.

Another important aspect of synchronizing with natural rhythms involves managing environmental temperature. Our bodies have built-in mechanisms to regulate temperature, striving to maintain equilibrium through sweating when hot and shivering when cold. However, modern conveniences like air conditioning and heating can sometimes disrupt these natural processes. By being mindful of our environmental conditions, we can support our body's natural regulation efforts.

For instance, dressing in layers allows you to adjust your clothing based on the ambient temperature, helping you stay comfortable without relying excessively on artificial climate control. Utilizing natural ventilation by opening windows can also improve indoor air quality and promote a healthier living environment. Furthermore, maintaining a consistent and comfortable sleep environment by keeping your bedroom cool can aid in achieving restful sleep, which is crucial for overall health.

Choosing non-toxic ingredients in your daily life is another key component of supporting long-term health. In today's market, many products contain chemicals that can be harmful over time. From cleaning supplies and personal care items to food and beverages, being selective about what you bring into your home can minimize exposure to potentially dangerous substances.

Opt for natural and organic products where possible. For example, using natural cleaners like vinegar and baking soda can replace chemical-laden alternatives. When it comes to personal care, look for items free from parabens, phthalates, and synthetic fragrances. Additionally, prioritize whole, unprocessed foods and avoid those with artificial additives or preservatives. Reading labels and educating yourself about common toxic ingredients can empower you to make healthier choices, fostering an environment that supports well-being.

Incorporating restorative practices such as mindful breathing and relaxation techniques is essential for maintaining balance and reducing stress. The constant demands of modern life can lead to chronic stress, negatively impacting both physical and mental health. Mindful breathing exercises are simple yet powerful tools to calm the mind and body. Practicing deep, slow breaths can activate the parasympathetic nervous system, promoting relaxation and reducing stress hormones like cortisol.

Various techniques like diaphragmatic breathing, box breathing, and alternate nostril breathing can be easily integrated into daily life. To practice diaphragmatic breathing, find a comfortable position and place one hand on your chest and the other on your abdomen. Inhale deeply through your nose, allowing your diaphragm to expand and your abdomen to rise. Exhale slowly through your mouth, feeling your abdomen fall. Repeat this cycle several times, focusing on the rhythm of your breath.

Relaxation techniques, such as progressive muscle relaxation, guided imagery, and yoga, also play a vital role in restoring balance. Progressive muscle relaxation involves systematically tensing and relaxing different muscle groups, which helps release physical tension and promote a sense of calm. Guided imagery uses visualization to create soothing mental images, transporting you to a peaceful place and reducing stress. Yoga combines physical postures, breath control, and meditation, offering a holistic approach to relaxation.

Integrating these practices into a busy lifestyle may seem challenging, but even short sessions can yield significant benefits. Start with just a few minutes a day and gradually increase the duration as you become more comfortable. Creating a dedicated space for relaxation at home can also encourage regular practice. Whether it's a quiet corner for meditation, a cozy spot for reading, or a mat for yoga, having a designated area can signal to your mind and body that it's time to unwind.

BRINGING IT ALL TOGETHER

In this chapter, we have explored the significance of aligning with our natural rhythms for improved well-being. By understanding the circadian rhythm and how it regulates various bodily functions, such as sleep-wake cycles, digestion, and energy levels, we can make informed choices that enhance our overall health. Consistent meal times, timed physical activities, and recognizing periods of peak energy and low energy help maintain a balanced lifestyle. Adhering to these natural cues supports better metabolic function, improved digestion, and enhanced mental and physical stamina.

Additionally, we discussed the importance of addressing disruptions to the circadian rhythm, which can significantly impact health. Irregular sleep patterns or inconsistent eating habits can lead to adverse effects like obesity, insomnia, and reduced cognitive function. Implementing strategies like organized meal schedules, planned physical activities, and minimizing exposures that disrupt natural rhythms can foster an environment conducive to optimal health. By aligning our daily routines with our body's natural clock, we promote a harmonious and healthier way of living.

CHAPTER 5: LIVING WITH VIBRANT ENERGY

Living with vibrant energy is an achievable goal that encompasses more than just physical fitness. It is about nurturing a fearless mindset and adopting habits that enhance overall vitality and health. Fear, often a significant barrier to achieving our highest potential, can drain energy and redirect focus away from growth and wellness. By understanding the nature of fear and learning how to manage it effectively, individuals can unlock an enduring sense of fearlessness that fuels their energy levels. This chapter delves into practical strategies for overcoming fear and maintaining a resilient disposition that supports vibrant living.

Readers will explore various techniques such as mindfulness practices, exposure therapy, and the cultivation of a positive mindset to mitigate the impacts of fear. Real-life examples of renowned figures who have harnessed fearless energy, along with scientific insights, illustrate the transformative power of these approaches. Additionally, the chapter outlines holistic methods to achieve peak health and vitality, including balanced nutrition, regular physical activity, adequate sleep, preventive medical care, and strong social connections. Together, these elements form a comprehensive guide to living with vibrant energy, enabling readers to integrate healthier habits into their daily routines for sustained well-being.

FEARLESS ENERGY

Understanding the nature of fear and its impact on energy levels is fundamental to cultivating fearless energy. Fear is a natural response to perceived threats, rooted in our evolutionary past. While it once served as a crucial survival mechanism, modern-day fears often stem from social situations, financial concerns, or health anxieties. When unchecked, fear can wreak havoc on our energy levels by triggering stress responses that deplete our physical and mental stamina. The constant state of alertness and anxiety diverts energy away from productive pursuits and into maintaining a state of readiness for threats, whether real or imagined.

One effective technique for overcoming fear involves practicing mindfulness. Mindfulness encourages living in the present moment and observing thoughts without judgment. By staying grounded in the now, individuals can detach from fear-driven narratives about the future or regrets about the past. Techniques like breathing exercises, body scans, and mindful meditation help calm the mind and reduce the physiological symptoms of fear, such as increased heart rate and tension. Over time, mindfulness can rewire how people respond to fear, making them less reactive and more composed.

Another powerful approach to diminishing fear's grip is exposure therapy. This therapeutic method involves gradually confronting the feared object or situation in a controlled and systematic manner. Starting with the least frightening scenarios, individuals build up to more challenging ones, allowing them to desensitize themselves to the fear stimulus over time. For instance, someone with a fear of public speaking might start by talking in front of a small group of friends and progressively work up to larger audiences. By repeatedly facing their fears, individuals learn that the anticipated negative outcomes are often unfounded, which significantly reduces the fear's intensity.

A positive mindset plays a pivotal role in maintaining fearless energy. Cultivating a positive outlook involves shifting focus from potential failures to possibilities and opportunities. Positive affirmations, goal setting, and focusing on past successes can reinforce this mindset. Surrounding oneself with supportive and encouraging individuals further strengthens one's capacity to maintain positivity. A positive mindset empowers individuals to view challenges as temporary setbacks rather than insurmountable obstacles, fueling them with the energy required to pursue their goals.

Real-life examples provide compelling evidence of the transformative power of cultivating fearless energy. Consider the story of Nelson Mandela, who spent 27 years in prison under an oppressive regime. Despite extreme adversity, Mandela maintained an unwavering sense of purpose and utilized his time to reflect, educate himself, and prepare for future leadership. His ability to overcome fear and stay optimistic fueled his mission and ultimately led to the dismantling of apartheid in South Africa. Similarly, Oprah Winfrey's journey from a troubled childhood to becoming a media mogul showcases how a resilient, fearless mindset can lead to extraordinary achievements. Winfrey has frequently spoken about using mindfulness practices and maintaining a positive outlook to navigate her fears and achieve her dreams.

Likewise, J.K. Rowling faced numerous rejections before publishing the Harry Potter series, yet she persisted despite her fears of failure. Through determination and resilience, Rowling transformed her initial setbacks into one of the most successful literary franchises in history. Her story emphasizes the importance of embracing challenges with a fearless attitude.

In addition to these individual stories, scientific studies have shown the benefits of a positive mindset and mindfulness in reducing fear and enhancing energy levels. Research indicates that regular mindfulness practice can lower cortisol levels, which are often elevated due to chronic fear and stress. Lower cortisol levels correspond with improved mood, better sleep quality, and higher overall energy levels, contributing to a sustained state of vitality.

Furthermore, integrating these techniques and perspectives requires consistency and dedication. Establishing daily mindfulness routines, engaging in cognitive-behavioral practices, and surrounding oneself with positive influences are all steps toward fostering a fearless, energetic life. It is essential to remember that progress may be gradual, but each step taken towards managing fear builds a stronger foundation for fearless energy.

ACHIEVING THE HIGHEST LEVELS OF HEALTH AND VITALITY

Achieving peak health and vitality is a multifaceted endeavor that requires a holistic approach. At its core, it involves adopting balanced nutrition, maintaining regular exercise, prioritizing sleep, and integrating preventive medical care. Additionally, nurturing mental health through practices like meditation and stress management, along with fostering strong social connections, plays a crucial role in this pursuit.

Balanced nutrition is the foundation of good health. Consuming a variety of foods rich in essential nutrients ensures that the body receives the vitamins and minerals it needs to function optimally. Fruits and vegetables are packed with antioxidants, which help combat oxidative stress and inflammation. Proteins from lean meats, beans, and nuts support muscle repair and growth, while healthy fats from sources like avocados and olive oil are vital for brain health. A diet rich in whole grains, such as brown rice and quinoa, provides sustained energy throughout the day. By focusing on nutrient-dense foods, individuals can maintain a stable metabolism and reduce the risk of chronic diseases.

Regular physical activity is another cornerstone of vibrant health. Exercise not only strengthens muscles and bones but also boosts cardiovascular health. Engaging in moderate aerobic activities, like walking, cycling, or swimming, for at least 150 minutes per week can improve heart health and increase endurance. Strength training exercises, performed two or more days a week, enhance muscle mass and bone density, reducing the risk of osteoporosis. Furthermore, physical activity releases endorphins, the body's natural mood lifters, which can help alleviate symptoms of depression and anxiety.

Equally important as nutrition and exercise is ensuring adequate sleep. Sleep is the body's natural way of repairing and rejuvenating itself. Adults typically need seven to nine hours of quality sleep each night. Poor sleep can lead to weight gain, weakened immunity, and reduced cognitive function. Establishing a regular sleep schedule, creating a restful environment, and avoiding stimulants like caffeine before bed can improve sleep quality. Prioritizing sleep helps in maintaining energy levels, enhancing memory, and supporting overall health.

Preventive care and regular medical check-ups are essential components of achieving peak vitality. Regular visits to healthcare professionals enable early detection and management of potential health issues. Screenings for blood pressure, cholesterol, diabetes, and cancer can catch problems before they become serious. Vaccinations help protect against preventable diseases. Routine dental and eye exams ensure oral and visual health. Preventive care not only extends lifespan but also enhances quality of life by preventing complications from untreated conditions.

Mental health is intricately connected to physical well-being. Integrating practices like meditation, mindfulness, and stress management into daily routines can significantly impact health. Meditation involves focusing on the present moment, which can reduce stress and promote relaxation. Mindfulness practices, such as deep-breathing exercises and yoga, enhance emotional regulation and decrease anxiety. Stress management techniques, including time management and setting realistic goals, can help individuals handle life's challenges more effectively. By cultivating a calm mind, individuals can better cope with stressors and maintain a positive outlook, which contributes to overall vitality.

In addition to individual practices, the role of community and social connections cannot be overstated. Humans are inherently social beings, and meaningful relationships contribute to mental and emotional health. Strong social networks provide support during difficult times, offer a sense of belonging, and reduce feelings of loneliness. Participating in community activities, volunteering, and maintaining close relationships with family and friends can enhance life satisfaction and resilience. Moreover, social connections can encourage healthy behaviors by providing motivation and accountability.

BRINGING IT ALL TOGETHER

In this chapter, we explored the concept of fearless energy and its crucial role in achieving optimal health and vitality. By understanding fear's impact on our energy levels and employing techniques such as mindfulness and exposure therapy, individuals can learn to manage their fears effectively. Mindfulness promotes present-moment awareness, reducing stress-related fatigue, while exposure therapy helps desensitize fear responses through gradual confrontation. These methods, combined with a positive mindset, empower individuals to face challenges head-on and maintain high energy levels.

We also discussed practical strategies for attaining the highest levels of health and vitality through balanced nutrition, regular exercise, adequate sleep, and preventive medical care. A well-rounded diet rich in essential nutrients supports overall bodily function, while consistent physical activity enhances cardiovascular and muscular health. Quality sleep is vital for recovery and mental clarity, and preventive healthcare ensures early detection of potential issues. Integrating mental health practices and fostering strong social connections further bolster these efforts, creating a comprehensive approach to sustained wellness and fearless energy.

CHAPTER 6: BREAKFASTS TO KICKSTART YOUR METABOLIC ENGINE: ENERGIZING RECIPES

As dawn breaks and the world slowly stirs into motion, there's nothing quite like the promise of a nourishing breakfast to properly fuel the start of a new day. Imagine opening your morning with a Spiced Apple & Quinoa Breakfast Bowl, where each spoonful is a warm hug of cinnamon-spiced apples paired with protein-rich quinoa, setting a comforting tone for the morning.

Envision yourself savoring Avocado & Egg Toast with Tomato Salsa, where creamy avocado slices and a perfectly cooked egg sit atop a crispy toast, draped in a zesty tomato salsa that awakens all your senses. Or dive into a Berry & Yogurt Smoothie Bowl, bursting with the bright colors and sweet tastes of fresh berries, blended into a silky smooth yogurt that energizes your spirit as much as your metabolism.

Each recipe in this chapter is designed to bring a sparkle to your morning routine, turning the first meal of the day into a delightful ritual that celebrates fresh ingredients and invigorating flavors. From the hearty Sweet Potato & Black Bean Breakfast Burritos offering a fulfilling start to busy mornings, to the light and refreshing Greek Yogurt Parfait with Honey Roasted Figs, these breakfasts are tailored to enhance your energy levels, boost your health, and prepare you for the challenges ahead.

Step into your kitchen and let these recipes transform your morning meals into a cornerstone of daily success and vitality, ensuring that every day begins with not just good food, but great energy.

SPICED APPLE & QUINOA BREAKFAST BOWL

Servings

2

Preparation Time

10 minutes

Cooking Time

15 minutes

INGREDIENTS:

- 1 cup quinoa, rinsed
- 2 cups water
- 2 medium apples, diced
- 1 teaspoon cinnamon
- 1/2 teaspoon nutmeg
- 1/4 cup walnuts, chopped
- 2 tablespoons chia seeds
- 1 tablespoon honey or maple syrup (optional)
- 1/4 cup almond milk or milk of choice

INSTRUCTIONS:

1. **Cook Quinoa:** In a medium saucepan, combine rinsed quinoa and water. Bring to a boil, then reduce heat to low, cover, and simmer for about 15 minutes, or until the quinoa is fluffy and water is absorbed.
2. **Spice the Apples:** While the quinoa is cooking, add diced apples to a separate pan over medium heat. Sprinkle with cinnamon and nutmeg, stirring occasionally, until the apples are slightly softened and fragrant, about 5 minutes.
3. **Toast Walnuts:** In a small skillet, toast the chopped walnuts over medium heat for about 3-4 minutes, stirring frequently until they are golden and aromatic. Remove from heat.
4. **Mix Ingredients:** Once the quinoa is cooked, stir in the spiced apples, toasted walnuts, and chia seeds. Drizzle with honey or maple syrup for a touch of sweetness if desired.
5. **Serve with Milk:** Divide the quinoa mixture into bowls and pour over with almond milk. Serve warm.

AVOCADO & EGG BREAKFAST BOWLS WITH TOMATO SALSA

Servings

2

Preparation Time

10 minutes

Cooking Time

15 minutes

INGREDIENTS:

- 1 ripe avocado, peeled and mashed
- 4 eggs
- 1 small tomato, finely choppe
- 1/4 red onion, finely chopped
- 1 tablespoon chopped cilantro
- Juice of 1 lime
- Salt and pepper to taste
- 1 tablespoon olive oil

INSTRUCTIONS:

1. **Prepare Salsa:** In a small bowl, combine chopped tomato, red onion, cilantro, lime juice, salt, and pepper. Mix well and set aside.
2. **Cook Eggs:** Heat olive oil in a skillet over medium heat. Crack the eggs and cook to desired doneness, either scrambled or sunny-side up.
3. **Assemble Bowls:** Divide the mashed avocado between two bowls. Place two cooked eggs in each bowl on top of the avocado.
4. **Serve:** Spoon fresh tomato salsa over the eggs and avocado. Serve immediately.

BERRY & YOGURT SMOOTHIE BOWL

Servings

2

Preparation Time

5 minutes

Cooking Time

0 minutes

INGREDIENTS:

- 1 cup Greek yogurt
- 1/2 cup frozen mixed berries (blueberries, raspberries, strawberries)
- 1 banana, sliced
- 1 tablespoon flaxseeds
- 1 tablespoon honey (optional)
- A handful of granola
- A few almonds, chopped

INSTRUCTIONS:

1. **Blend Smoothie:** In a blender, combine Greek yogurt, frozen berries, banana, flaxseeds, and honey if using. Blend until smooth.
2. **Serve:** Pour the smoothie mixture into bowls. Top with granola and chopped almonds. Enjoy immediately.

SPINACH & FETA OMELETTE

Servings

2

Preparation Time

5 minutes

Cooking Time

10 minutes

INGREDIENTS:

- 4 eggs
- 1 cup fresh spinach, chopped
- 1/2 cup feta cheese, crumbled
- 2 tablespoons milk
- Salt and pepper to taste
- 1 tablespoon olive oil

INSTRUCTIONS:

1. **Prepare Omelette Mixture:** In a bowl, whisk together eggs, milk, salt, and pepper.
2. **Cook Spinach:** Heat olive oil in a skillet over medium heat. Add spinach and sauté until wilted, about 2 minutes.
3. **Add Egg Mixture:** Pour the egg mixture over the spinach in the skillet. Sprinkle feta cheese on top.
4. **Cook Omelette:** Let the eggs cook undisturbed until the edges start to lift from the pan. Fold the omelette in half and continue cooking until the eggs are set.
5. **Serve:** Slide the omelette onto a plate and serve hot.

SWEET POTATO & BLACK BEAN BREAKFAST BURRITOS

Servings	Preparation Time	Cooking Time
2	15 minutes	20 minutes

INGREDIENTS:

- 2 medium sweet potatoes, peeled and diced
- 1 can black beans, drained and rinsed
- 4 whole wheat tortillas
- 1 avocado, sliced
- 1/2 cup cheddar cheese, shredded
- 1 teaspoon cumin
- 1/2 teaspoon paprika
- Salt and pepper to taste
- 1 tablespoon olive oil

INSTRUCTIONS:

1. **Cook Sweet Potatoes:** Heat olive oil in a skillet over medium heat. Add diced sweet potatoes, cumin, paprika, salt, and pepper. Cook until sweet potatoes are tender, about 15 minutes.
2. **Assemble Burritos:** Warm the tortillas in a microwave or on a skillet. Lay each tortilla flat and distribute the sweet potato mixture, black beans, avocado slices, and shredded cheese among them.
3. **Roll Burritos:** Fold the sides of the tortilla and roll tightly.
4. **Serve:** Serve the burritos warm, with salsa or sour cream if desired.

OVERNIGHT CHIA & OATS PUDDING

Servings	Preparation Time	Cooking Time
2	10 minutes (plus overnight soaking)	0 minutes

INGREDIENTS:

- 1/4 cup chia seeds
- 1/4 cup rolled oats
- 1 cup almond milk
- 1 tablespoon maple syrup
- 1/2 teaspoon vanilla extract
- Fresh fruits for topping (banana, kiwi, berries)

INSTRUCTIONS:

1. **Mix Ingredients:** In a bowl, mix together chia seeds, rolled oats, almond milk, maple syrup, and vanilla extract.
2. **Refrigerate:** Cover the bowl and refrigerate overnight.
3. **Serve:** The next morning, stir the pudding well. If it's too thick, add a little more almond milk. Top with fresh fruits and serve.

COCONUT & ALMOND PORRIDGE

Servings	Preparation Time	Cooking Time
2	5 minutes	10 minutes

INGREDIENTS:

- 1 cup steel-cut oats
- 2 cups coconut milk
- 1/4 cup sliced almonds
- 1/4 cup shredded coconut
- 2 tablespoons honey or maple syrup
- 1/2 teaspoon cinnamon
- Fresh berries for topping

INSTRUCTIONS:

1. **Cook Oats:** In a medium saucepan, bring coconut milk to a boil. Add steel-cut oats and reduce heat to a simmer. Cook for about 10 minutes, stirring occasionally, until the oats are soft and creamy.
2. **Add Flavors:** Stir in the sliced almonds, shredded coconut, and cinnamon. Sweeten with honey or maple syrup to taste.
3. **Serve:** Spoon the porridge into bowls and top with fresh berries. Serve warm for a cozy start to your day.

GREEK YOGURT WITH HONEY ROASTED FIGS

Servings	Preparation Time	Cooking Time
2	5 minutes	15 minutes

INSTRUCTIONS:

1. **Roast Figs:** Preheat your oven to 375°F (190°C). Place fig halves on a baking sheet, drizzle with 2 tablespoons of honey, and sprinkle with cardamom. Roast for about 15 minutes, or until juicy and slightly caramelized.
2. **Prepare Yogurt:** In bowls, divide the Greek yogurt.
3. **Serve:** Top each bowl of yogurt with roasted figs, a drizzle of the remaining honey, and a sprinkle of chopped pistachios.

INGREDIENTS:

- 4 fresh figs, halved
- 2 cups Greek yogurt
- 4 tablespoons honey, divided
- 1/2 teaspoon ground cardamom
- A handful of pistachios, chopped

SAVORY BREAKFAST MUFFINS

Servings
6 muffins

Preparation Time

10 minutes

Cooking Time
20 minutes

INGREDIENTS:

- 1 cup whole wheat flour
- 1/2 cup oats
- 2 teaspoons baking powder
- 1/4 teaspoon salt
- 1/2 cup milk
- 2 eggs
- 1/4 cup olive oil
- 1/2 cup grated zucchini
- 1/2 cup grated carrot
- 1/4 cup chopped spring onions
- 1/2 cup shredded cheddar cheese

INSTRUCTIONS:

1. **Preheat Oven & Prep Muffin Tin:** Preheat oven to 350°F (175°C). Grease a muffin tin or line with muffin papers.
2. **Combine Dry Ingredients:** In a large bowl, mix together flour, oats, baking powder, and salt.
3. **Add Wet Ingredients:** In another bowl, beat together milk, eggs, and olive oil. Stir this into the dry ingredients until just combined. Fold in zucchini, carrot, spring onions, and cheese.
4. **Bake:** Spoon the batter into the prepared muffin tin. Bake for about 20 minutes, or until a toothpick inserted into the center comes out clean.
5. **Serve:** Allow to cool slightly before serving. Enjoy warm.

AVOCADO AND SALMON BREAKFAST SALAD

Servings
2

Preparation Time

10 minutes

Cooking Time
0 minutes

INGREDIENTS:

- 2 cups mixed greens (spinach, arugula, kale)
- 1 ripe avocado, sliced
- 4 ounces smoked salmon
- 1 small cucumber, sliced
- 2 tablespoons olive oil
- Juice of 1 lemon
- Salt and pepper to taste
- 1 tablespoon capers

INSTRUCTIONS:

1. **Assemble Salad:** In a large bowl, combine mixed greens, avocado slices, smoked salmon, and cucumber.
2. **Dress Salad:** Whisk together olive oil, lemon juice, salt, and pepper. Drizzle over the salad.
3. **Garnish and Serve:** Sprinkle capers over the top and serve immediately for a fresh, energizing breakfast.

POMEGRANATE & WALNUT OATMEAL

Servings
2

Preparation Time
5 minutes

Cooking Time
5 minutes

INGREDIENTS:

- 1 cup rolled oats
- 2 cups water or milk
- 1/2 cup pomegranate seeds
- 1/4 cup walnuts, chopped
- 1 tablespoon honey or maple syrup
- 1/2 teaspoon vanilla extract
- Pinch of salt

INSTRUCTIONS:

1. **Cook Oatmeal:** In a saucepan, bring water or milk to a boil. Add oats and salt, reduce heat, and simmer until oats are tender, about 5 minutes.
2. **Add Flavors:** Stir in vanilla extract and sweeten with honey or maple syrup.
3. **Serve:** Divide oatmeal between bowls. Top with pomegranate seeds and chopped walnuts. Serve warm for a nutritious and tasty start to the day.

PEAR AND GINGER PORRIDGE

Servings
2

Preparation Time
5 minutes

Cooking Time
15 minutes

INGREDIENTS:

- 1 cup steel-cut oats
- 2 cups water or milk
- 1 ripe pear, diced
- 1 teaspoon fresh ginger, grated
- 2 tablespoons chopped walnuts
- 1 tablespoon honey or maple syrup
- Pinch of cinnamon

INSTRUCTIONS:

1. **Cook Oats:** In a saucepan, bring water or milk to a boil. Add steel-cut oats and simmer on low heat, stirring occasionally, until oats are tender, about 15 minutes.
2. **Add Flavors:** Halfway through cooking, add the diced pear and grated ginger to the oats. Stir well to combine.
3. **Finish & Serve:** Once the oats are cooked, stir in cinnamon and sweeten with honey or maple syrup. Garnish with chopped walnuts and serve warm for a comforting and energizing breakfast.

ZUCCHINI AND HERB FRITTATA

Servings	Preparation Time	Cooking Time
4	10 minutes	20 minutes

INGREDIENTS:

- 6 eggs
- 1 medium zucchini, grated and excess moisture squeezed out
- 1/4 cup fresh herbs (parsley, chives, basil), chopped
- 1/4 cup feta cheese, crumbled
- Salt and pepper to taste
- 1 tablespoon olive oil

INSTRUCTIONS:

1. **Preheat Oven:** Preheat your oven to 375°F (190°C).
2. **Prepare Egg Mixture:** In a bowl, whisk together eggs, salt, and pepper. Stir in the grated zucchini, fresh herbs, and crumbled feta cheese.
3. **Cook Frittata:** Heat olive oil in an oven-safe skillet over medium heat. Pour in the egg mixture and cook for about 5 minutes until the edges begin to set. Transfer the skillet to the oven and bake for 15 minutes, or until the frittata is fully set.
4. **Serve:** Let the frittata cool for a few minutes before slicing and serving. Enjoy a herby, nutritious start to your day.

TROPICAL SMOOTHIE BOWL

Servings	Preparation Time	Cooking Time
2	5 minutes	0 minutes

INGREDIENTS:

- 1 cup frozen mango chunks
- 1 banana
- 1/2 cup coconut milk
- 1/2 teaspoon turmeric powder
- 1 tablespoon chia seeds
- Fresh kiwi, sliced
- Unsweetened coconut flakes
- Almond slivers

INSTRUCTIONS:

1. **Blend Smoothie:** In a blender, combine frozen mango, banana, coconut milk, and turmeric powder. Blend until smooth.
2. **Prepare Bowl:** Pour the smoothie into bowls. Top with sliced kiwi, coconut flakes, chia seeds, and almond slivers.
3. **Serve:** Enjoy immediately for a bright, energizing breakfast loaded with antioxidants and healthy fats.

SAVORY OATMEAL WITH POACHED EGG

Servings

2
muffins

Preparation Time

5 minutes

Cooking Time

10 minutes

INGREDIENTS:

- 1 cup rolled oats
- 2 cups water or broth
- 1 teaspoon soy sauce
- 1/4 teaspoon black pepper
- 2 eggs
- 1 green onion, chopped
- 1 tablespoon olive oil
- Sriracha or hot sauce, for serving

INSTRUCTIONS:

1. **Cook Oatmeal:** In a saucepan, bring water or broth to a boil. Add oats, soy sauce, and black pepper. Reduce heat to a simmer and cook until oats are tender, about 5-7 minutes.
2. **Poach Eggs:** While oats are cooking, poach eggs in a separate pot of simmering water until whites are set but yolks are still runny, about 3-4 minutes.
3. **Assemble & Serve:** Spoon the savory oatmeal into bowls. Top each serving with a poached egg and chopped green onions. Drizzle with olive oil and add a dash of hot sauce for extra flavor.

BLUEBERRY ALMOND OVERNIGHT OATS

Servings

2

Preparation Time

5 minutes
(plus overnight refrigeration)

INGREDIENTS:

- 1 cup rolled oats
- 1 cup unsweetened almond milk
- 1/2 cup blueberries (fresh or frozen)
- 2 tablespoons chia seeds
- 2 tablespoons sliced almonds
- 2 tablespoons honey or maple syrup
- 1/2 teaspoon vanilla extract

INSTRUCTIONS:

1. **Combine Ingredients:** In a mason jar or bowl, mix together the oats, almond milk, blueberries, chia seeds, almonds, honey, and vanilla extract.
2. **Refrigerate Overnight:** Cover and refrigerate overnight to allow the oats to absorb the liquid and soften.
3. **Serve:** Stir the oats in the morning before serving. Add a little more almond milk if the mixture is too thick. Enjoy this energizing breakfast that provides a balanced mix of carbs, protein, and healthy fats.

BAKED AVOCADO EGGS WITH FRESH SALSA

Servings	Preparation Time	Cooking Time
2	5 minutes	15 minutes

INGREDIENTS:

- 2 ripe avocados
- 4 eggs
- Salt and freshly ground black pepper, to taste
- 1 small tomato, diced
- 1/4 red onion, diced
- 1 jalapeño, seeded and finely chopped (optional)
- Juice of 1 lime
- Fresh cilantro, chopped for garnish

INSTRUCTIONS:

1. **Preheat Oven:** Set your oven to 425°F (220°C).
2. **Prepare Avocado:** Slice avocados in half and remove pits. Scoop out a bit more avocado to enlarge the center hole. Place them in a baking dish to keep them stable.
3. **Add Eggs:** Crack an egg into the center of each avocado half. Season with salt and pepper.
4. **Bake:** Place in the oven and bake for about 15 minutes, or until the eggs are cooked to your liking.
5. **Prepare Salsa:** While the avocados are baking, combine diced tomato, red onion, jalapeño (if using), and lime juice in a small bowl. Season with salt to taste.
6. **Serve:** Remove avocados from the oven, spoon fresh salsa over them, and garnish with cilantro. Serve immediately.

AVOCADO AND SMOKED SALMON BREAKFAST BOWLS

Servings	Preparation Time
2	5 minutes

INGREDIENTS:

- 1 ripe avocado
- 4 oz smoked salmon
- 1 tablespoon lemon juice
- Fresh dill for garnish
- Salt and pepper to taste

INSTRUCTIONS:

1. **Prepare Avocado:** In a bowl, mash the avocado with lemon juice, salt, and pepper until smooth.
2. **Assemble Bowls:** Divide the mashed avocado evenly between two bowls. Arrange the smoked salmon neatly over the avocado.
3. **Garnish and Serve:** Garnish each bowl with fresh dill. Enjoy this nutritious dish that's rich in omega-3 fatty acids and healthy fats, ideal for boosting brain function and maintaining energy levels throughout the morning.

GREEK YOGURT PARFAIT WITH HONEY AND NUTS

Servings

1

Preparation Time

5 minutes

INSTRUCTIONS:

1. **Layer Parfait:** In a glass or bowl, layer Greek yogurt, honey, chopped nuts, and berries if using.
2. **Repeat Layers:** Continue layering until all ingredients are used.
3. **Serve:** Enjoy immediately or chill in the refrigerator for an hour before serving. This parfait is a great source of protein and healthy fats, ideal for a sustained energy release.

INGREDIENTS:

- 1 cup Greek yogurt
- 2 tablespoons honey
- 1/4 cup mixed nuts (walnuts, almonds, pecans), chopped
- 1/4 cup mixed berries (optional)

SWEET POTATO AND BLACK BEAN BREAKFAST BURRITO

Servings

2

Preparation Time

10 minutes

Cooking Time

15 minutes

INSTRUCTIONS:

1. **Cook Sweet Potato:** Heat olive oil in a skillet over medium heat. Add diced sweet potato, paprika, salt, and pepper. Cook until tender, about 10 minutes.
2. **Add Eggs and Beans:** Add beaten eggs and black beans to the skillet. Stir until the eggs are cooked through.
3. **Assemble Burritos:** Spoon the mixture onto corn tortillas.
4. **Serve:** Roll up the tortillas, cut in half, and serve warm. Enjoy this hearty breakfast packed with fiber and protein, perfect for a high-energy start to the day.

INGREDIENTS:

- 1 medium sweet potato, peeled and diced
- 1/2 cup black beans, drained and rinsed
- 2 corn tortillas
- 2 eggs, beaten
- 1/4 teaspoon paprika
- Salt and pepper to taste
- 1 tablespoon olive oil

CHAPTER 7: ENERGIZING LUNCHES FOR SUSTAINED MIDDAY VITALITY: NUTRITIOUS RECIPES

Imagine a midday meal as a vibrant oasis of flavors that not only delights your palate but also recharges your body's energy reserves. In this chapter, we dive into the world of energizing lunches designed to elevate your noon-time dining experience with dishes that combine zest, zeal, and nourishing ingredients. Each recipe is a crafted symphony of tastes that ensures your lunch break is anything but ordinary.

Picture yourself unwinding with a Lemon Garlic Salmon Salad that blends the refreshing zest of lemon with the rich, omega-packed succulence of salmon, or savor the robust flavors of a Grilled Chicken and Quinoa Bowl, where every bite offers a burst of protein and complex carbs. Feel the crunch and freshness of a Beetroot and Goat Cheese Arugula Salad, where earthy beets meet creamy goat cheese on a bed of peppery arugula, drizzled with a balsamic reduction that dances on your taste buds.

From the heartiness of a Sweet Potato & Black Bean Burrito to the light, crisp textures of Spicy Tofu Lettuce Wraps, these recipes are tailored to boost your energy without the post-lunch lethargy. Each dish is not just a meal but an experience that sustains you through the day, keeping you focused, productive, and vibrant.

Step into the delightful world of lunches that aren't just meant to satisfy hunger but to revitalize your spirit and body, making every lunch hour a cherished energizing ritual.

LEMON GARLIC SALMON SALAD

Servings	Preparation Time	Cooking Time
2	10 minutes	15 minutes

INGREDIENTS:

- 2 salmon fillets (6 oz each)
- 4 cups mixed greens (such as arugula, spinach, and romaine)
- 1/2 cup cherry tomatoes, halved
- 1/4 red onion, thinly sliced
- 1/4 cup cucumber, sliced
- 2 tablespoons olive oil
- Juice of 1 lemon
- 2 cloves garlic, minced
- Salt and pepper to taste
- 1 tablespoon fresh dill, chopped

INSTRUCTIONS:

1. **Prep Salmon:** Preheat oven to 400°F (200°C). Place salmon on a baking sheet lined with parchment paper. Drizzle with 1 tablespoon olive oil, half the lemon juice, minced garlic, and season with salt and pepper.
2. **Cook Salmon:** Bake for 12-15 minutes, or until salmon is cooked through and flakes easily with a fork.
3. **Assemble Salad:** In a large bowl, toss mixed greens, cherry tomatoes, red onion, and cucumber.
4. **Make Dressing:** Whisk together the remaining olive oil and lemon juice, season with salt, pepper, and dill.
5. **Serve:** Place salad on plates, top with cooked salmon, and drizzle with lemon dill dressing.

GRILLED CHICKEN AND QUINOA BOWL

Servings	Preparation Time	Cooking Time
2	20 minutes	10 minutes

INGREDIENTS:

- 2 chicken breasts
- 1 cup quinoa
- 2 cups water
- 1 avocado, diced
- 1/2 cup corn kernels
- 1/2 cup black beans, rinsed and drained
- 1 lime, juiced
- 2 tablespoons cilantro, chopped
- Salt and pepper to taste
- 1 tablespoon olive oil

INSTRUCTIONS:

1. **Cook Quinoa:** Rinse quinoa under cold water. In a saucepan, bring water to a boil, add quinoa, reduce heat to low, cover, and simmer for 15 minutes. Let stand for 5 minutes, then fluff with a fork.
2. **Grill Chicken:** Season chicken breasts with salt and pepper. Grill over medium heat for 5-7 minutes on each side until cooked through. Let rest for a few minutes before slicing.
3. **Assemble Bowl:** In bowls, layer cooked quinoa, sliced chicken, avocado, corn, and black beans.
4. **Add Dressing:** Drizzle with lime juice and olive oil, then sprinkle with chopped cilantro.
5. **Serve:** Enjoy a balanced and flavorful bowl that's perfect for a high-energy lunch.

BEEF AND BROCCOLI STIR-FRY

Servings

2

Preparation Time

10 minutes

Cooking Time

10 minutes

INGREDIENTS:

- 1/2 lb beef sirloin, thinly sliced
- 2 cups broccoli florets
- 1 bell pepper, sliced
- 2 cloves garlic, minced
- 2 tablespoons soy sauce (or gluten-free tamari)
- 1 tablespoon sesame oil
- 1 teaspoon cornstarch
- 1/2 cup beef broth
- Salt and pepper to taste

INSTRUCTIONS:

1. **Prep Sauce:** In a small bowl, mix soy sauce, sesame oil, cornstarch, and beef broth.
2. **Cook Beef:** In a large skillet or wok, heat a bit of oil over high heat. Add beef and stir-fry until it starts to brown, about 3-4 minutes. Remove and set aside.
3. **Cook Vegetables:** In the same skillet, add a bit more oil if needed, then add broccoli, bell pepper, and garlic. Stir-fry until vegetables are just tender.
4. **Combine:** Return beef to the skillet, pour in the sauce, and cook together for another 2-3 minutes until the sauce thickens.
5. **Serve:** Season with salt and pepper. Serve hot, ideally over a bed of rice or noodles for a complete meal.

TUNA NICOISE SALAD

Servings

2

Preparation Time

20 minutes

INGREDIENTS:

- 2 tuna steaks (6 oz each)
- 4 cups mixed salad greens
- 1/2 cup green beans, blanched
- 1/2 cup small potatoes, boiled and halved
- 1/4 cup olives, pitted
- 2 hard-boiled eggs, quartered
- 1/4 red onion, thinly sliced
- For the dressing:
  - 1/4 cup olive oil
  - 2 tablespoons red wine vinegar
  - 1 teaspoon Dijon mustard
  - Salt and pepper to taste

INSTRUCTIONS:

1. **Grill Tuna:** Season tuna steaks with salt and pepper. Grill over high heat for 2-3 minutes per side (or to desired doneness).
2. **Prepare Dressing:** Whisk together olive oil, red wine vinegar, Dijon mustard, salt, and pepper.
3. **Assemble Salad:** On plates, arrange salad greens, green beans, potatoes, olives, eggs, and red onion. Top with grilled tuna, sliced or left whole.
4. **Dress and Serve:** Drizzle the dressing over the salad and serve immediately.

SHRIMP AND AVOCADO TACO SALAD

Servings	Preparation Time	Cooking Time
2	15 minutes	5 minutes

INGREDIENTS:

- 1/2 lb shrimp, peeled and deveined
- 4 cups romaine lettuce, chopped
- 1 avocado, diced
- 1/2 cup cherry tomatoes, halved
- 1/4 cup red onion, finely chopped
- 1/4 cup cilantro, chopped
- Juice of 1 lime
- 2 tablespoons olive oil
- 1 teaspoon chili powder
- Salt and pepper to taste

INSTRUCTIONS:

1. **Cook Shrimp:** In a skillet, heat 1 tablespoon olive oil over medium heat. Add shrimp, sprinkle with chili powder, salt, and pepper. Cook until shrimp are pink and opaque, about 3-5 minutes.
2. **Prepare Salad:** In a large bowl, toss romaine lettuce, avocado, cherry tomatoes, red onion, and cilantro.
3. **Dress Salad:** Drizzle with lime juice and the remaining olive oil. Toss to coat.
4. **Add Shrimp:** Top the salad with cooked shrimp.
5. **Serve:** Enjoy a refreshing and protein-rich salad that's perfect for a quick, nourishing lunch.

MEDITERRANEAN TUNA SALAD

Servings	Preparation Time	Cooking Time
2	10 minutes	0 minutes

INGREDIENTS:

- 1 can of tuna in olive oil, drained
- 1/2 cup diced cucumber
- 1/2 cup halved cherry tomatoes
- 1/4 cup diced red onion
- 1/4 cup Kalamata olives, pitted and halved
- 1/4 cup crumbled feta cheese
- Juice of 1 lemon
- 2 tablespoons extra virgin olive oil
- Salt and pepper to taste
- Fresh parsley, chopped

INSTRUCTIONS:

1. **Combine Ingredients:** In a large bowl, mix tuna, cucumber, cherry tomatoes, red onion, Kalamata olives, and feta cheese.
2. **Dress the Salad:** Drizzle with lemon juice and olive oil. Toss to combine. Season with salt and pepper.
3. **Serve:** Garnish with fresh parsley before serving. This salad can be served on its own or over a bed of fresh greens.

SWEET POTATO & BLACK BEAN BURRITO

Servings	Preparation Time	Cooking Time
2	15 minutes	20 minutes

INSTRUCTIONS:

1. **Roast Sweet Potatoes:** Preheat oven to 400°F (200°C). Toss diced sweet potatoes with olive oil, cumin, and chili powder. Spread on a baking sheet and roast for 20 minutes, or until tender.
2. **Assemble Burritos:** Lay out the tortillas and distribute roasted sweet potatoes and black beans evenly among them. Top with grated cheese.
3. **Roll and Serve:** Roll up the tortillas tightly, wrap in foil if taking to-go, or serve immediately with a dollop of sour cream and salsa.

INGREDIENTS:

- 2 medium sweet potatoes, peeled and diced
- 1 can black beans, drained and rinsed
- 1 teaspoon cumin
- 1/2 teaspoon chili powder
- 2 corn tortillas
- 1/2 cup grated cheese (cheddar or Monterey Jack)
- 1/4 cup sour cream
- 1/4 cup salsa
- 2 tablespoons olive oil

ASIAN-STYLE SHRIMP AND RICE NOODLE BOWL

Servings	Preparation Time	Cooking Time
2	10 minutes	10 minutes

INSTRUCTIONS:

1. **Cook Noodles:** Prepare rice noodles according to package instructions. Drain and set aside.
2. **Sauté Shrimp:** In a skillet, heat sesame oil over medium heat. Add shrimp and cook until pink, about 2-3 minutes per side. Remove and set aside.
3. **Stir-Fry Vegetables:** In the same skillet, add snap peas, carrot, and bell pepper. Stir-fry for about 3 minutes. Add garlic and ginger and cook for another minute.
4. **Combine:** Return shrimp to the skillet along with cooked noodles. Add soy sauce and honey. Toss everything to coat and heat through.
5. **Serve:** Garnish with green onions and sesame seeds before serving.

INGREDIENTS:

- 4 oz rice noodles
- 12 large shrimp, peeled and deveined
- 1 cup snap peas, trimmed
- 1 carrot, julienned
- 1 bell pepper, thinly sliced
- 2 green onions, sliced
- 1/4 cup soy sauce
- 1 tablespoon sesame oil
- 1 tablespoon honey
- 1 garlic clove, minced
- 1 teaspoon grated ginger
- Sesame seeds for garnish

BEEF AND VEGETABLE SKILLET

Servings
4

Preparation Time
10 minutes

Cooking Time
30 minutes

INGREDIENTS:

- 1 lb (450 g) beef sirloin, thinly sliced
- 2 tablespoons olive oil
- 1 red bell pepper, sliced
- 1 yellow bell pepper, sliced
- 1 large onion, sliced
- 2 cloves garlic, minced
- 1 teaspoon smoked paprika
- 1/2 teaspoon ground cumin
- Salt and freshly ground black pepper, to taste
- 1/4 cup beef broth (ensure it's gluten-free)
- 2 tablespoons fresh parsley, chopped

INSTRUCTIONS:

1. **Heat Skillet:** In a large skillet, heat 1 tablespoon of olive oil over medium-high heat.
2. **Cook Beef:** Add the beef slices to the skillet and sear until browned on both sides and cooked through, about 3-4 minutes per side. Remove beef from skillet and set aside.
3. **Sauté Vegetables:** In the same skillet, add the remaining tablespoon of olive oil. Sauté the onions, bell peppers, and garlic until they begin to soften, about 5 minutes.
4. **Season:** Sprinkle smoked paprika, cumin, salt, and pepper over the vegetables, stirring to combine.
5. **Deglaze:** Pour beef broth into the skillet, stirring to lift any browned bits from the bottom of the pan. Allow the mixture to simmer for about 5 minutes, or until the vegetables are tender and the liquid has slightly reduced.
6. **Combine and Serve:** Return the cooked beef to the skillet, stir to combine with the vegetables, and heat through for a couple of minutes. Garnish with chopped parsley before serving.

CAPRESE QUINOA SALAD

Servings
2

Preparation Time
10 minutes

Cooking Time
10 minutes

INGREDIENTS:

- 1 cup quinoa, rinsed
- 2 cups water
- 1 cup cherry tomatoes, halved
- 1/2 cup fresh mozzarella balls, halved
- 1/4 cup fresh basil leaves, torn
- 2 tablespoons balsamic reduction
- 2 tablespoons olive oil
- Salt and pepper to taste

INSTRUCTIONS:

1. **Cook Quinoa:** In a saucepan, bring water to a boil. Add quinoa, reduce heat to low, cover, and simmer for 15 minutes or until quinoa is fluffy and water is absorbed.
2. **Prepare Salad:** In a large bowl, combine cooked quinoa, cherry tomatoes, mozzarella balls, and fresh basil. Drizzle with olive oil and balsamic reduction. Toss to combine.
3. **Season and Serve:** Season with salt and pepper to taste and serve immediately or chill in the refrigerator before serving for a refreshing lunch option.

BEETROOT AND GOAT CHEESE ARUGULA SALAD

 Servings
2

 Preparation Time
10 minutes

Cooking Time
0 minutes

INGREDIENTS:

- 2 cups arugula
- 1 medium beetroot, cooked and sliced
- 1/2 cup goat cheese, crumbled
- 1/4 cup walnuts, toasted and chopped
- 2 tablespoons olive oil
- 1 tablespoon balsamic vinegar
- Salt and pepper to taste
- Fresh mint, chopped (optional)

INSTRUCTIONS:

1. **Prepare the Salad:** In a large bowl, place the arugula as the base.
2. **Add Toppings:** Layer sliced beetroot, crumbled goat cheese, and toasted walnuts on top of the arugula.
3. **Dressing:** Drizzle olive oil and balsamic vinegar over the salad. Toss gently to coat everything evenly.
4. **Season:** Add salt and pepper to taste. Garnish with fresh mint for an extra burst of flavor.
5. **Serve:** Enjoy this colorful and vibrant salad that's perfect for a refreshing, light lunch.

CURRIED LENTIL SOUP

 Servings
4

 Preparation Time
10 minutes

 Cooking Time
25 minutes

INGREDIENTS:

- 1 cup red lentils
- 1 onion, chopped
- 2 carrots, diced
- 4 cups vegetable broth
- 1 can coconut milk
- 2 teaspoons curry powder
- 1 teaspoon turmeric
- Salt and pepper to taste
- 2 tablespoons olive oil
- Fresh cilantro for garnish

INSTRUCTIONS:

1. **Sauté Vegetables:** In a large pot, heat olive oil over medium heat. Add onions and carrots, cook until softened, about 5 minutes.
2. **Cook Lentils:** Add red lentils, curry powder, and turmeric to the pot. Stir to coat the lentils and vegetables in the spices.
3. **Simmer:** Pour in vegetable broth and bring to a boil. Reduce heat and simmer for 20 minutes, or until the lentils are tender.
4. **Add Coconut Milk:** Stir in coconut milk and heat through. Adjust seasoning with salt and pepper.
5. **Serve:** Ladle the soup into bowls and garnish with fresh cilantro. This warm, spicy soup is ideal for a comforting lunch.

SPICY CHICKPEA AND QUINOA BOWL

Servings	Preparation Time	Cooking Time
2	15 minutes	20 minutes

INGREDIENTS:

- 1 cup quinoa, rinsed
- 1 can (15 oz) chickpeas, drained and rinsed
- 1 avocado, sliced
- 1 small red onion, finely chopped
- 1 lime, juiced
- 1 teaspoon chili powder
- 1/2 teaspoon cumin
- 2 tablespoons olive oil
- Fresh cilantro, chopped
- Salt and pepper to taste

INSTRUCTIONS:

1. **Cook Quinoa:** In a saucepan, bring 2 cups of water to a boil. Add quinoa, reduce heat to low, cover, and cook for 15-20 minutes until fluffy.
2. **Season Chickpeas:** Toss chickpeas with chili powder, cumin, salt, and pepper.
3. **Sauté Chickpeas:** Heat 1 tablespoon olive oil in a skillet over medium heat. Add seasoned chickpeas and sauté until golden and crispy, about 8-10 minutes.
4. **Assemble Bowl:** Divide cooked quinoa between bowls, top with crispy chickpeas, sliced avocado, and chopped red onion. Drizzle with lime juice and the remaining olive oil.
5. **Serve:** Garnish with fresh cilantro before serving. This hearty bowl is perfect for a filling, flavorful lunch.

LEMON HERB GRILLED CHICKEN SALAD

Servings	Preparation Time	Cooking Time

2	10 minutes (plus marinating time)	10 minutes

INGREDIENTS:

- 2 chicken breasts
- Juice of 1 lemon
- 2 tablespoons olive oil
- 1 teaspoon dried herbs (thyme, basil, or oregano)
- Salt and pepper to taste
- Mixed greens (lettuce, arugula, spinach)
- 1/2 cup cherry tomatoes, halved
- 1/4 cup shaved Parmesan cheese

INSTRUCTIONS:

1. **Marinate Chicken:** In a bowl, mix lemon juice, olive oil, herbs, salt, and pepper. Add chicken breasts and marinate for at least 30 minutes.
2. **Grill Chicken:** Grill chicken over medium heat for about 5 minutes per side or until cooked through. Let rest for a few minutes, then slice.
3. **Prepare Salad:** On plates, arrange mixed greens and cherry tomatoes. Top with sliced grilled chicken and shaved Parmesan cheese.
4. **Serve:** Serve with additional lemon wedges or your favorite vinaigrette.

SPICY TOFU LETTUCE WRAPS

Servings
2

Preparation Time
15 minutes

Cooking Time
10 minutes

INGREDIENTS:

- 1 block firm tofu, drained and crumbled
- 1 head of lettuce (iceberg or butter lettuce works well)
- 1 carrot, julienned
- 1 bell pepper, thinly sliced
- 2 green onions, chopped
- 2 tablespoons soy sauce
- 1 tablespoon hoisin sauce
- 1 teaspoon chili sauce (adjust to taste)
- 1 tablespoon sesame oil
- 1 garlic clove, minced
- 1 teaspoon grated ginger

INSTRUCTIONS:

1. **Prepare Tofu:** Heat sesame oil in a pan over medium heat. Add minced garlic and grated ginger, sauté for a minute.
2. **Cook Tofu:** Add crumbled tofu to the pan, stir-fry for about 5 minutes until it starts to brown. Pour in soy sauce, hoisin sauce, and chili sauce. Cook for another 5 minutes until well combined and flavorful.
3. **Assemble Wraps:** Take leaves of lettuce, fill each with a scoop of the spicy tofu mixture, and top with julienned carrot, sliced bell pepper, and chopped green onions.
4. **Serve:** Enjoy these wraps as a crunchy, spicy, and satisfying midday meal.

SESAME SOBA NOODLE SALAD

Servings
2

Preparation Time
10 minutes

Cooking Time
5 minutes

INGREDIENTS:

- 4 oz soba noodles
- 1 carrot, julienned
- 1 cucumber, julienned
- 1/4 cup edamame, shelled
- 2 tablespoons sesame seeds
- 3 tablespoons soy sauce
- 1 tablespoon sesame oil
- 1 tablespoon honey
- 1 teaspoon fresh grated ginger
- Green onions, sliced, for garnish

INSTRUCTIONS:

1. **Cook Noodles:** Cook soba noodles according to package instructions, then rinse under cold water and drain.
2. **Prepare Salad:** In a large bowl, combine noodles, carrot, cucumber, and edamame.
3. **Make Dressing:** In a small bowl, whisk together soy sauce, sesame oil, honey, and ginger.
4. **Combine:** Pour dressing over noodle mixture and toss to coat evenly. Sprinkle with sesame seeds.
5. **Serve:** Garnish with sliced green onions and serve chilled. This dish is perfect for a refreshing and light lunch that keeps you fueled.

GARLIC HERB ROASTED CHICKEN WITH ROOT VEGETABLES

Servings	Preparation Time	Cooking Time

4	15 minutes	45 minutes

INGREDIENTS:

- 4 chicken breasts, bone-in and skin-on
- 1 tablespoon olive oil
- 4 cloves garlic, minced
- 1 teaspoon dried rosemary
- 1 teaspoon dried thyme
- Salt and freshly ground black pepper, to taste
- 3 carrots, peeled and chopped
- 2 parsnips, peeled and chopped
- 1 sweet potato, peeled and cubed
- Fresh parsley, chopped for garnish

INSTRUCTIONS:

1. **Preheat Oven:** Set your oven to 400°F (200°C).
2. **Prepare Chicken:** Rub each chicken breast with olive oil and then coat with minced garlic, rosemary, thyme, salt, and pepper.
3. **Arrange Vegetables:** In a roasting pan, mix carrots, parsnips, and sweet potato with a drizzle of olive oil and a sprinkle of salt and pepper. Place the seasoned chicken breasts on top of the vegetables.
4. **Roast:** Place in the oven and roast for approximately 45 minutes, or until the chicken is golden brown and reaches an internal temperature of 165°F (75°C), and the vegetables are tender.
5. **Garnish and Serve:** Remove from the oven, let rest for a few minutes, then garnish with fresh parsley before serving.

TURKEY AND CRANBERRY SALAD

Servings	Preparation Time	Cooking Time
2	10 minutes	0 minutes

INGREDIENTS:

- 2 cups mixed salad greens
- 1/2 pound cooked turkey breast, sliced
- 1/4 cup dried cranberries
- 1/4 cup pecans, toasted
- 1/4 cup crumbled goat cheese
- 2 tablespoons balsamic vinaigrette

INSTRUCTIONS:

1. **Prepare Salad:** In a large bowl, toss mixed greens with balsamic vinaigrette.
2. **Add Ingredients:** Add sliced turkey, dried cranberries, toasted pecans, and goat cheese to the greens.
3. **Toss and Serve:** Gently toss everything together to combine. Serve immediately for a sweet and savory lunch option that's quick and satisfying.

GRILLED TROUT WITH CITRUS HERB SALAD

 Servings

 Preparation Time

Cooking Time

2

10 minutes

10 minutes

INGREDIENTS:

- 2 trout fillets, about 6 oz each
- Salt and freshly ground black pepper, to taste
- 2 tablespoons olive oil
- 1 orange, segmented
- 1 grapefruit, segmented
- 1/4 cup thinly sliced red onion
- 1/4 cup fresh basil leaves, chopped
- 1/4 cup fresh mint leaves, chopped
- 2 tablespoons lemon juice
- Lemon wedges, for serving

INSTRUCTIONS:

1. **Preheat Grill:** Heat your grill to medium-high.
2. **Season Trout:** Brush trout fillets with 1 tablespoon olive oil and season with salt and pepper.
3. **Grill Trout:** Place fillets skin-side down on the grill. Cook for 4-5 minutes on each side or until the fish flakes easily with a fork.
4. **Prepare Citrus Herb Salad:** In a bowl, combine orange and grapefruit segments, red onion, basil, mint, and the remaining olive oil. Drizzle with lemon juice and toss gently.
5. **Serve:** Plate each grilled trout fillet and top with a generous amount of citrus herb salad. Serve with lemon wedges on the side.

LEMON PEPPER GRILLED FISH TACOS

 Servings

 Preparation Time

 Cooking Time

2

10 minutes

10 minutes

INGREDIENTS:

- 2 fish fillets (such as tilapia or cod)
- Juice of 1 lemon
- 1 teaspoon black pepper
- 1/2 teaspoon salt
- 4 small corn tortillas
- 1 cup shredded cabbage
- 1/4 cup plain yogurt
- 1 tablespoon mayonnaise
- 1 tablespoon chopped cilantro
- Lime wedges for serving

INSTRUCTIONS:

1. **Season Fish:** Sprinkle fish fillets with lemon juice, salt, and black pepper.
2. **Grill Fish:** Grill fish over medium heat for about 4-5 minutes per side, until cooked through and flaky.
3. **Prepare Sauce:** Mix yogurt, mayonnaise, and cilantro in a small bowl.
4. **Assemble Tacos:** Warm tortillas, place a piece of grilled fish on each, top with shredded cabbage, and drizzle with yogurt sauce.
5. **Serve:** Serve with lime wedges on the side for a zesty, refreshing lunch.

CHAPTER 8: DINNERS THAT RECHARGE AND HEAL: NOURISHING NIGHTTIME RECIPES

As the sun dips below the horizon and the evening settles in, it's time to unwind with dinners that do more than just satisfy hunger—they heal, rejuvenate, and restore. In this chapter, each recipe is a carefully crafted ritual, combining wholesome ingredients with rich flavors to nourish your body and soothe your soul.

Picture a plate of Ginger Turmeric Salmon, where each bite is infused with the warm, healing spices of turmeric and ginger, their anti-inflammatory powers mingling with the omega-rich succulence of salmon. This dish doesn't just feed your body; it cares for your wellbeing.

Imagine filling your kitchen with the aroma of Lemon Herb Roasted Chicken, its skin crisped to perfection, the meat succulent and tender, each forkful replete with the freshness of herbs and the zest of lemon, recharging your senses and your strength.

Visualize sitting down to a bowl of Butternut Squash Soup, the creamy texture and sweet, nutty flavor forming a comforting embrace that wards off the evening chill and fills you with warmth from the inside out.

Each dinner option, from the earthy richness of Vegan Lentil and Sweet Potato Shepherd's Pie to the zesty, heart-healthy Balsamic Glazed Salmon, is designed not just to end the day, but to enhance it, providing meals that support healing and energy replenishment.

These nighttime recipes are more than meals; they are a means to mend, a way to end each day with balance and vitality, ensuring that every dinner is not just eaten, but experienced—a perfect close to your daily journey of living vibrantly.

HERB-CRUSTED SALMON WITH ROASTED ASPARAGUS

Servings

4

Preparation Time

10 minutes

Cooking Time

20 minutes

INGREDIENTS:

- 4 salmon fillets (about 6 oz each)
- 1 tablespoon olive oil
- 1 teaspoon garlic powder
- 1 teaspoon dried dill
- 1 teaspoon dried parsley
- Salt and pepper to taste
- 1 bunch asparagus, trimmed
- 1 lemon, sliced for garnish
- Fresh dill for garnish

INSTRUCTIONS:

1. **Preheat Oven:** Set to 400°F (200°C).
2. **Prepare Salmon:** Rub each salmon fillet with olive oil and season with garlic powder, dried dill, dried parsley, salt, and pepper. Place on a lined baking sheet.
3. **Prepare Asparagus:** Toss asparagus with a little olive oil, salt, and pepper. Arrange around the salmon on the baking sheet.
4. **Roast:** Bake in the preheated oven for about 15-20 minutes, or until salmon is flaky and asparagus is tender.
5. **Serve:** Garnish salmon and asparagus with fresh lemon slices and a sprinkle of fresh dill.

LEMON HERB ROASTED CHICKEN

Servings

2

Preparation Time

15 minutes

Cooking Time

1 hour

INGREDIENTS:

- 1 whole chicken (about 4 lbs)
- 1 lemon, halved
- 1 tablespoon rosemary, chopped
- 1 tablespoon thyme, chopped
- 3 garlic cloves, minced
- 2 tablespoons olive oil
- Salt and pepper to taste

INSTRUCTIONS:

1. **Prepare Chicken:** Preheat oven to 425°F (220°C). Rub chicken with olive oil, garlic, rosemary, thyme, salt, and pepper. Place lemon halves inside the chicken cavity.
2. **Roast:** Place chicken in a roasting pan. Roast for about 1 hour, or until the juices run clear and a thermometer inserted into the thickest part of the thigh reads 165°F (75°C).
3. **Rest & Serve:** Let the chicken rest for 10 minutes before carving. Serve with roasted vegetables.

GINGER TURMERIC SALMON

Servings
2

Preparation Time
10 minutes

Cooking Time
20 minutes

INGREDIENTS:

- 2 salmon fillets (6 oz each)
- 1 tablespoon grated fresh ginger
- 1 teaspoon turmeric
- 1 garlic clove, minced
- 2 tablespoons soy sauce
- 2 tablespoons olive oil
- 1 tablespoon honey
- Salt and pepper to taste
- Fresh cilantro for garnish

INSTRUCTIONS:

1. **Marinate Salmon:** In a bowl, mix together ginger, turmeric, garlic, soy sauce, olive oil, and honey. Place salmon in the marinade, ensuring each piece is well coated. Let sit for at least 30 minutes in the refrigerator.
2. **Cook Salmon:** Preheat oven to 375°F (190°C). Place salmon on a baking sheet lined with parchment paper. Bake for 15-20 minutes, or until cooked through.
3. **Serve:** Season with salt and pepper, garnish with fresh cilantro, and serve with a side of steamed vegetables.

QUINOA STUFFED BELL PEPPERS

Servings
4

Preparation Time
15 minutes

Cooking Time
30 minutes

INGREDIENTS:

- 4 bell peppers, tops cut off and seeds removed
- 1 cup quinoa, cooked
- 1 can (15 oz) black beans, drained and rinsed
- 1 cup corn kernels
- 1/2 cup tomatoes, chopped
- 1/2 cup onions, chopped
- 1 teaspoon cumin
- 1/2 teaspoon chili powder
- 1/2 cup shredded cheddar cheese
- Salt and pepper to taste

INSTRUCTIONS:

1. **Prepare Peppers:** Preheat oven to 350°F (175°C). Arrange bell peppers in a baking dish.
2. **Make Filling:** In a bowl, mix together cooked quinoa, black beans, corn, tomatoes, onions, cumin, and chili powder. Season with salt and pepper.
3. **Stuff Peppers:** Spoon the filling into each bell pepper. Top with shredded cheese.
4. **Bake:** Cover with foil and bake for 30 minutes, until peppers are tender.
5. **Serve:** Serve hot, with a side salad or garlic bread.

THAI COCONUT CURRY WITH TOFU

Servings
4

Preparation Time
15 minutes

Cooking Time
20 minutes

INGREDIENTS:

- 14 oz firm tofu, cubed
- 1 tablespoon coconut oil
- 1 onion, sliced
- 2 bell peppers, sliced
- 1 zucchini, sliced
- 2 tablespoons red curry paste
- 1 can (14 oz) coconut milk
- 1 tablespoon soy sauce
- 1 tablespoon sugar
- Juice of 1 lime
- Fresh basil leaves, for garnish

INSTRUCTIONS:

1. **Prepare Tofu:** In a skillet, heat coconut oil over medium heat. Add tofu cubes and fry until golden on all sides. Remove from skillet and set aside.
2. **Cook Vegetables:** In the same skillet, add onion, bell peppers, and zucchini. Sauté until softened.
3. **Add Curry:** Stir in red curry paste and cook for 1 minute until fragrant. Pour in coconut milk, soy sauce, and sugar. Bring to a simmer.
4. **Combine:** Return tofu to the skillet. Simmer everything together for 10 minutes.
5. **Serve:** Finish with lime juice and garnish with fresh basil. Serve over steamed rice or noodles.

BUTTERNUT SQUASH SOUP

Servings
4

Preparation Time
10 minutes

Cooking Time
30 minutes

INGREDIENTS:

- 1 butternut squash, peeled and cubed
- 1 onion, chopped
- 2 garlic cloves, minced
- 4 cups vegetable broth
- 1 teaspoon cinnamon
- 1/2 teaspoon nutmeg
- 2 tablespoons olive oil
- Salt and pepper to taste
- Pumpkin seeds for garnish

INSTRUCTIONS:

1. **Sauté Onions:** In a large pot, heat olive oil over medium heat. Add onions and garlic, sauté until soft.
2. **Cook Squash:** Add butternut squash, vegetable broth, cinnamon, and nutmeg. Bring to a boil, then reduce heat and simmer for 20 minutes, until squash is tender.
3. **Blend:** Use an immersion blender to puree the soup until smooth.
4. **Season & Serve:** Season with salt and pepper. Serve hot, garnished with pumpkin seeds.

BAKED LEMON PEPPER COD

Servings	Preparation Time	Cooking Time
4	5 minutes	15 minutes

INGREDIENTS:

- 4 cod fillets
- 2 lemons, sliced
- 4 tablespoons olive oil
- 1 tablespoon lemon pepper seasoning
- Fresh parsley, chopped for garnish

INSTRUCTIONS:

1. **Preheat Oven:** Preheat oven to 400°F (200°C).
2. **Prepare Cod:** Place cod fillets on a baking sheet lined with parchment paper. Drizzle with olive oil and sprinkle with lemon pepper seasoning. Top with lemon slices.
3. **Bake:** Bake for 12-15 minutes, or until cod is flaky and cooked through.
4. **Serve:** Garnish with fresh parsley and serve with a side of steamed vegetables or a salad.

ROASTED TURMERIC CAULIFLOWER WITH CHICKPEAS AND QUINOA

Servings	Preparation Time	Cooking Time
4	15 minutes	30 minutes

INGREDIENTS:

- 1 large head of cauliflower, cut into florets
- 1 can (15 oz) chickpeas, drained, rinsed, and patted dry
- 1 cup quinoa
- 2 cups vegetable broth
- 2 tablespoons olive oil
- 1 teaspoon ground turmeric
- 1/2 teaspoon ground cumin
- 1/4 teaspoon cayenne pepper (optional, adjust to taste)
- Salt and pepper to taste
- 1/2 cup chopped parsley
- Juice of 1 lemon
- 1/4 cup toasted almonds, chopped

INSTRUCTIONS:

1. **Preheat Oven:** Preheat your oven to 400°F (200°C). Line a baking sheet with parchment paper.
2. **Season Cauliflower and Chickpeas:** In a large bowl, combine the cauliflower florets and chickpeas. Drizzle with olive oil, then sprinkle with turmeric, cumin, cayenne pepper, salt, and pepper. Toss well to ensure all pieces are evenly coated with the spices and oil.
3. **Roast:** Spread the cauliflower and chickpeas on the prepared baking sheet in a single layer. Roast in the preheated oven for about 25-30 minutes, or until the cauliflower is tender and golden.
4. **Cook Quinoa:** While the vegetables are roasting, rinse quinoa under cold water. In a medium saucepan, bring the vegetable broth to a boil. Add quinoa, reduce heat to low, cover, and simmer for 15 minutes, or until all the liquid is absorbed. Remove from heat and let sit, covered, for 5 minutes. Fluff with a fork.
5. **Combine:** In a large serving bowl, combine the roasted cauliflower and chickpeas with the cooked quinoa. Drizzle with lemon juice and toss to mix.
6. **Garnish and Serve:** Sprinkle with chopped parsley and toasted almonds before serving.

MOROCCAN CHICKPEA STEW

Servings

4

Preparation Time

10 minutes

Cooking Time

25 minutes

INGREDIENTS:

- 1 tablespoon olive oil
- 1 onion, chopped
- 2 garlic cloves, minced
- 1 carrot, diced
- 1 can (15 oz) chickpeas, drained and rinsed
- 1 can (14 oz) diced tomatoes
- 2 cups vegetable broth
- 1 teaspoon cumin
- 1/2 teaspoon cinnamon
- 1/2 teaspoon paprika
- Salt and pepper to taste
- Fresh cilantro, for garnish

INSTRUCTIONS:

1. **Sauté Aromatics:** In a large pot, heat olive oil over medium heat. Add onion and garlic, cook until softened.
2. **Add Spices and Vegetables:** Stir in cumin, cinnamon, and paprika. Add carrot, chickpeas, and diced tomatoes. Cook for a few minutes to blend flavors.
3. **Simmer:** Pour in vegetable broth. Bring to a boil, then reduce heat and simmer for 20 minutes.
4. **Serve:** Season with salt and pepper. Garnish with fresh cilantro. Serve hot, perhaps with a side of couscous or bread.

GRILLED VEGETABLE AND HALLOUMI SKEWERS

Servings

4

Preparation Time

20 minutes

Cooking Time

10 minutes

INGREDIENTS:

- 1 zucchini, sliced into rounds
- 1 bell pepper, cut into pieces
- 1 red onion, cut into wedges
- 8 oz halloumi cheese, cut into cubes
- 2 tablespoons olive oil
- 1 tablespoon balsamic vinegar
- Salt and pepper to taste
- Fresh mint, for garnish

INSTRUCTIONS:

1. **Preheat Grill:** Preheat grill to medium-high heat.
2. **Prepare Skewers:** Thread zucchini, bell pepper, onion, and halloumi cubes alternately onto skewers.
3. **Season:** Drizzle skewers with olive oil and balsamic vinegar. Season with salt and pepper.
4. **Grill:** Grill skewers for 8-10 minutes, turning occasionally, until vegetables are tender and halloumi is golden.
5. **Serve:** Garnish with fresh mint. Serve with a drizzle of extra balsamic if desired.

SPINACH AND RICOTTA STUFFED CHICKEN

Servings

4

Preparation Time

20 minutes

Cooking Time
25 minutes

INGREDIENTS:

- 4 boneless, skinless chicken breasts
- 1 cup ricotta cheese
- 1 cup fresh spinach, chopped
- 2 cloves garlic, minced
- 1/2 cup grated Parmesan cheese
- Salt and pepper to taste
- 2 tablespoons olive oil
- Fresh lemon wedges for serving

INSTRUCTIONS:

1. **Prepare Chicken:** Preheat oven to 375°F (190°C). Make a deep cut along the side of each chicken breast to create a pocket.
2. **Mix Filling:** In a bowl, combine ricotta, spinach, garlic, and Parmesan. Season with salt and pepper.
3. **Stuff Chicken:** Spoon the ricotta mixture into each chicken pocket. Secure with toothpicks if necessary.
4. **Cook Chicken:** Heat olive oil in a large oven-proof skillet over medium heat. Sear chicken on both sides until golden, about 3 minutes per side. Transfer skillet to oven and bake for 20 minutes, or until chicken is cooked through.
5. **Serve:** Remove toothpicks, squeeze fresh lemon over the chicken, and serve with a side of roasted vegetables or a garden salad.

VEGAN LENTIL AND SWEET POTATO SHEPHERD'S PIE

Servings
Servings: 6

Preparation Time

30 minutes

Cooking Time

30 minutes

INGREDIENTS:

- 2 cups lentils, cooked
- 2 large sweet potatoes, peeled and cubed
- 1 onion, diced
- 2 carrots, diced
- 2 celery stalks, diced
- 3 cloves garlic, minced
- 1 cup vegetable broth
- 2 tablespoons tomato paste
- 1 teaspoon thyme
- 1/2 teaspoon rosemary
- Salt and pepper to taste
- 2 tablespoons olive oil
- 1/4 cup almond milk

INSTRUCTIONS:

1. **Preheat Oven:** Preheat oven to 400°F (200°C).
2. **Cook Vegetables:** In a skillet, heat olive oil over medium heat. Add onion, carrots, celery, and garlic. Cook until softened, about 10 minutes.
3. **Make Lentil Mixture:** Add cooked lentils, vegetable broth, tomato paste, thyme, and rosemary to the skillet. Simmer for 10 minutes, until thickened. Season with salt and pepper.
4. **Prepare Sweet Potato Mash:** Boil sweet potatoes until tender, about 15 minutes. Drain and mash with almond milk, salt, and pepper until smooth.
5. **Assemble and Bake:** Spoon lentil mixture into a baking dish. Top with sweet potato mash. Bake for 20 minutes or until the top is slightly crispy.
6. **Serve:** Let cool slightly before serving. Enjoy a hearty, plant-based meal.

BALSAMIC GLAZED SALMON

Servings
4

Preparation Time

10 minutes

Cooking Time
20 minutes

INGREDIENTS:

- 4 salmon fillets
- 1/4 cup balsamic vinegar
- 2 tablespoons honey
- 1 tablespoon Dijon mustard
- 1 garlic clove, minced
- Salt and pepper to taste
- 2 tablespoons olive oil
- Fresh parsley, chopped for garnish

INSTRUCTIONS:

1. **Preheat Oven:** Preheat oven to 400°F (200°C).
2. **Prepare Glaze:** In a small bowl, whisk together balsamic vinegar, honey, Dijon mustard, and garlic. Season with salt and pepper.
3. **Cook Salmon:** Place salmon fillets on a lined baking sheet. Brush with olive oil and season with salt and pepper. Bake for 10 minutes.
4. **Add Glaze:** Remove salmon from oven, brush with balsamic glaze, and return to oven. Bake for another 10 minutes or until glaze is caramelized and salmon is cooked through.
5. **Serve:** Garnish with fresh parsley and serve with steamed green beans or a fresh salad.

ROASTED CAULIFLOWER STEAK WITH TURMERIC AND TAHINI

Servings
4

Preparation Time

10 minutes

Cooking Time

25 minutes

INGREDIENTS:

- 2 large heads of cauliflower
- 2 tablespoons olive oil
- 1 teaspoon turmeric
- Salt and pepper to taste
- 1/4 cup tahini
- 1 lemon, juiced
- 1 tablespoon water
- Fresh herbs for garnish (parsley or cilantro)

INSTRUCTIONS:

1. **Preheat Oven:** Preheat oven to 400°F (200°C).
2. **Prepare Cauliflower:** Slice cauliflower heads into 1-inch thick steaks. Place on a baking sheet. Drizzle with olive oil and sprinkle with turmeric, salt, and pepper.
3. **Roast:** Roast in the oven for 25 minutes, flipping halfway through, until golden and tender.
4. **Make Tahini Sauce:** Whisk together tahini, lemon juice, and water until smooth.
5. **Serve:** Drizzle tahini sauce over cauliflower steaks and garnish with fresh herbs.

STIR-FRIED TOFU WITH BROCCOLI AND BELL PEPPER

Servings

4

Preparation Time

15 minutes

Cooking Time

10 minutes

INGREDIENTS:

- 14 oz firm tofu, pressed and cubed
- 1 head broccoli, cut into florets
- 1 red bell pepper, sliced
- 1 onion, sliced
- 2 cloves garlic, minced
- 2 tablespoons soy sauce
- 1 tablespoon sesame oil
- 1 teaspoon cornstarch
- 2 tablespoons water
- 1 tablespoon vegetable oil
- Sesame seeds for garnish

INSTRUCTIONS:

1. **Prepare Tofu:** In a bowl, toss tofu with cornstarch until evenly coated.
2. **Cook Tofu:** Heat vegetable oil in a large skillet or wok over medium-high heat. Add tofu and fry until golden on all sides. Remove from skillet and set aside.
3. **Stir-Fry Vegetables:** In the same skillet, add sesame oil. Sauté garlic, onion, broccoli, and bell pepper until vegetables are just tender.
4. **Combine:** Return tofu to the skillet. Add soy sauce and water. Cook, stirring frequently, for a few minutes until sauce is thickened and everything is heated through.
5. **Serve:** Garnish with sesame seeds. Serve hot with steamed rice or noodles.

HERB-ROASTED CHICKEN WITH ROOT VEGETABLES

Servings

4

Preparation Time

20 minutes

Cooking Time

1 hour

INGREDIENTS:

- 1 whole chicken (about 4 lbs)
- 1 lb mixed root vegetables (carrots, parsnips, turnips), peeled and chopped
- 1 onion, quartered
- 4 cloves garlic, minced
- 2 tablespoons fresh rosemary, chopped
- 2 tablespoons fresh thyme, chopped
- 3 tablespoons olive oil
- Salt and pepper to taste

INSTRUCTIONS:

1. **Preheat Oven:** Preheat oven to 425°F (220°C).
2. **Prepare Chicken:** Rub the chicken with 1 tablespoon olive oil, salt, pepper, and half of the herbs. Stuff the cavity with onion quarters and minced garlic.
3. **Roast Vegetables:** Toss the root vegetables with the remaining olive oil, herbs, salt, and pepper. Spread around the chicken in a roasting pan.
4. **Roast:** Place the chicken in the oven and roast for about 1 hour, or until the juices run clear and a thermometer inserted into the thickest part of the thigh reads 165°F (74°C).
5. **Serve:** Let the chicken rest for 10 minutes before carving. Serve with the roasted vegetables.

COCONUT SHRIMP CURRY

Servings	Preparation Time	Cooking Time
4	15 minutes	20 minutes

INGREDIENTS:

- 1 lb shrimp, peeled and deveined
- 1 can (14 oz) coconut milk
- 1 tablespoon curry powder
- 1 red bell pepper, sliced
- 1 onion, chopped
- 2 cloves garlic, minced
- 1 teaspoon ginger, minced
- 1 tablespoon olive oil
- Fresh cilantro, for garnish
- Salt to taste

INSTRUCTIONS:

1. **Sauté Aromatics:** In a large skillet, heat olive oil over medium heat. Add onion, garlic, and ginger, cooking until onion is translucent.
2. **Add Spices:** Stir in curry powder and cook for 1 minute until fragrant.
3. **Cook Shrimp:** Add shrimp and red bell pepper to the skillet, cook until shrimp starts to turn pink.
4. **Simmer:** Pour in coconut milk, bring to a simmer, and cook for 10 minutes, or until shrimp is fully cooked and sauce has thickened.
5. **Serve:** Season with salt, garnish with fresh cilantro, and serve over steamed rice or with naan bread.

LEMON BASIL ORZO WITH GRILLED VEGETABLES

Servings	Preparation Time	Cooking Time
4	15 minutes	15 minutes

INGREDIENTS:

- 1 cup orzo pasta
- 2 zucchinis, sliced lengthwise
- 1 red onion, sliced into rings
- 1 red bell pepper, sliced
- 2 tablespoons olive oil
- Juice and zest of 1 lemon
- 1/4 cup fresh basil, chopped
- Salt and pepper to taste
- Feta cheese, crumbled (optional)

INSTRUCTIONS:

1. **Cook Orzo:** Cook orzo according to package instructions. Drain and set aside.
2. **Grill Vegetables:** Brush vegetables with 1 tablespoon olive oil and grill over medium heat until charred and tender.
3. **Prepare Dressing:** In a large bowl, whisk together the remaining olive oil, lemon juice, lemon zest, and chopped basil.
4. **Combine:** Toss the cooked orzo and grilled vegetables in the lemon basil dressing. Season with salt and pepper.
5. **Serve:** Sprinkle with crumbled feta cheese if desired and serve warm or at room temperature.

EGGPLANT PARMESAN

Servings	Preparation Time	Cooking Time
4	20 minutes	30 minutes

INGREDIENTS:

- 2 large eggplants, sliced into 1/2-inch thick rounds
- 2 cups marinara sauce
- 2 cups mozzarella cheese, shredded
- 1/2 cup Parmesan cheese, grated
- 1 cup flour
- 2 eggs, beaten
- 2 cups breadcrumbs
- Salt and pepper to taste
- Olive oil for frying
- Fresh basil for garnish

INSTRUCTIONS:

1. **Prepare Eggplant:** Season eggplant slices with salt and let sit for 20 minutes. Pat dry with paper towels.
2. **Bread Eggplant:** Dredge each slice first in flour, then dip in beaten eggs, and finally coat with breadcrumbs.
3. **Fry Eggplant:** In a large skillet, heat olive oil over medium heat. Fry eggplant slices until golden on both sides. Drain on paper towels.
4. **Assemble:** In a baking dish, spread a layer of marinara sauce. Layer fried eggplant slices, top with mozzarella, and sprinkle with Parmesan. Repeat layers until all ingredients are used.
5. **Bake:** Preheat oven to 375°F (190°C). Bake for 30 minutes, or until cheese is bubbly and golden.
6. **Serve:** Garnish with fresh basil and serve hot.

GRILLED HALIBUT WITH MANGO SALSA

Servings
Servings: 4

Preparation Time

20 minutes

Cooking Time

10 minutes

INGREDIENTS:

- 4 halibut fillets (about 6 oz each)
- 2 tablespoons olive oil
- Juice of 1 lemon
- Salt and pepper to taste
- 1 ripe mango, peeled and diced
- 1/2 red bell pepper, finely chopped
- 1/4 cup red onion, finely chopped
- 1 small jalapeño, seeded and finely chopped (optional)
- Juice of 1 lime
- 2 tablespoons chopped fresh cilantro
- Salt to taste

INSTRUCTIONS:

1. **Prepare Mango Salsa:** In a medium bowl, combine diced mango, red bell pepper, red onion, jalapeño (if using), lime juice, and cilantro. Mix well. Season with salt to taste and set aside to let the flavors meld while you grill the fish.
2. **Grill the Halibut:** Preheat grill to medium-high heat. Pat the halibut fillets dry with paper towels. Brush each fillet with olive oil and squeeze lemon juice over them. Season with salt and pepper. Place fillets on the grill and cook for about 4-5 minutes on each side, or until the fish flakes easily with a fork and has nice grill marks.
3. **Enjoy:** Serve the grilled halibut fillets immediately, topped with a generous amount of mango salsa.

CHAPTER 9: PLANT-BASED AND VEGAN MEALS RECIPES

Envision a world where every meal is an expression of care and compassion, not just for our bodies but for the planet. Chapter 9 is dedicated to plant-based and vegan meals that are crafted with a deep respect for nature and an emphasis on sustainability. Each recipe is a celebration of the earth's bounty, offering dishes that are as kind to the environment as they are nourishing to your body.

Imagine the rich, earthy flavors of Vegan Portobello Mushroom Steaks, grilled to perfection and seasoned with herbs that highlight their natural juiciness. Picture the vibrant colors and spicy aromas of a Spicy Thai Peanut Sweet Potato Bowl, where each spoonful is a tapestry of textures and tastes that delight the senses.

Delight in the simplicity and sophistication of a Vegan Mushroom Risotto, creamy and comforting, with each grain of rice carrying the deep, umami flavors of mushrooms. Visualize wrapping your hands around a warm, soft taco filled with black beans and ripe avocado slices from our Black Bean and Avocado Tacos, where freshness meets flavor in every bite.

Each dish in this chapter—from the soothing warmth of Creamy Vegan Cauliflower Soup to the robust and satisfying Spicy Black Bean and Quinoa Burgers—is designed not only to fill the stomach but also to fulfill the soul's craving for meals that matter. These recipes are not merely food; they are a form of activism, a daily decision to choose sustainability and health without sacrificing flavor or fulfillment.

Step into the pages of this chapter and be inspired to transform your eating habits into a powerful statement of your values, with meals that promise vitality, variety, and a vision of a better world.

VEGAN PORTOBELLO MUSHROOM STEAKS

Servings

Preparation Time

Cooking Time

4 **15 minutes** **25 minutes**

INGREDIENTS:

- 4 large Portobello mushrooms, stems removed
- 1/4 cup balsamic vinegar
- 1/4 cup soy sauce (or tamari for a gluten-free option)
- 2 tablespoons olive oil
- 2 cloves garlic, minced
- 1 teaspoon smoked paprika
- 1 teaspoon dried thyme
- 1/2 teaspoon black pepper
- Fresh parsley, chopped for garnish
- Optional sides: Mashed potatoes or steamed green vegetables

INSTRUCTIONS:

1. **Marinate Mushrooms:** In a small bowl, whisk together balsamic vinegar, soy sauce, olive oil, minced garlic, smoked paprika, thyme, and black pepper. Place the mushrooms in a shallow dish, gill-side up. Pour the marinade over the mushrooms, ensuring they are well coated. Let them marinate for at least 15 minutes, or longer for deeper flavor.
2. **Preheat Oven:** Preheat your oven to 400°F (200°C).
3. **Bake Mushrooms:** Transfer the marinated mushrooms to a baking sheet lined with parchment paper. Reserve the marinade for basting. Bake for 25 minutes, basting halfway through with the reserved marinade.
4. **Prepare Sides:** While the mushrooms are baking, prepare your chosen sides, such as mashed potatoes or steamed vegetables.
5. **Serve:** Once the mushrooms are tender and flavorful, remove them from the oven. Place each mushroom steak on a plate, spooning any remaining juices from the baking sheet over them. Garnish with fresh parsley.
6. **Enjoy:** Serve immediately with your prepared sides for a complete, satisfying meal.

BLACK BEAN AND AVOCADO TACOS

Servings

Preparation Time

Cooking Time

4 **10 minutes** **10 minutes**

INGREDIENTS:

- 1 can (15 oz) black beans, drained and rinsed
- 2 avocados, diced
- 1/2 red onion, finely chopped
- Juice of 1 lime
- 1 teaspoon chili powder
- Salt and pepper to taste
- 8 corn tortillas
- Fresh cilantro for garnish
- Salsa for serving

INSTRUCTIONS:

1. **Prepare Filling:** In a bowl, mix black beans, avocado, red onion, lime juice, chili powder, salt, and pepper.
2. **Warm Tortillas:** Heat tortillas in a skillet or microwave until warm and pliable.
3. **Assemble Tacos:** Spoon the bean and avocado mixture into tortillas.
4. **Garnish:** Top with fresh cilantro and salsa.

VEGAN MUSHROOM RISOTTO

Servings	Preparation Time	Cooking Time
4	10 minutes	25 minutes

INGREDIENTS:

- 1 cup Arborio rice
- 3 cups vegetable broth, warmed
- 1 onion, chopped
- 2 cloves garlic, minced
- 2 cups mushrooms, sliced
- 1/2 cup white wine (optional)
- 2 tablespoons nutritional yeast
- 2 tablespoons olive oil
- Salt and black pepper to taste
- Fresh parsley for garnish

INSTRUCTIONS:

1. **Sauté Onion and Garlic:** In a large skillet, heat olive oil over medium heat. Add onion and garlic, sauté until translucent.
2. **Add Mushrooms:** Add mushrooms and cook until they begin to release their juices.
3. **Cook Rice:** Stir in Arborio rice and cook for a minute. Pour in white wine (if using) and let it evaporate.
4. **Add Broth Gradually:** Add warm vegetable broth one ladle at a time, stirring constantly, until the liquid is absorbed before adding more. Continue until the rice is creamy and al dente.
5. **Season:** Stir in nutritional yeast, salt, and pepper.
6. **Serve:** Garnish with fresh parsley and serve warm.

SPICY THAI PEANUT SWEET POTATO BOWL

Servings

Servings: 4

Preparation Time

15 minutes

Cooking Time

30 minutes

INGREDIENTS:

- 2 large sweet potatoes, peeled and cubed
- 1 bell pepper, sliced
- 1 broccoli crown, cut into florets
- 1 cup cooked quinoa
- 1/4 cup peanut butter
- 2 tablespoons soy sauce
- 1 tablespoon maple syrup
- 1 tablespoon lime juice
- 1 teaspoon grated ginger
- 1 clove garlic, minced
- 1/2 teaspoon chili flakes
- 2 tablespoons water
- 2 tablespoons chopped peanuts for garnish
- Fresh cilantro for garnish
- Olive oil

INSTRUCTIONS:

1. **Roast Vegetables:** Preheat oven to 400°F (200°C). Toss sweet potatoes, bell pepper, and broccoli with olive oil and spread on a baking sheet. Roast for 25-30 minutes, until tender and slightly caramelized.
2. **Prepare Sauce:** In a small bowl, whisk together peanut butter, soy sauce, maple syrup, lime juice, ginger, garlic, chili flakes, and water until smooth.
3. **Assemble Bowls:** Divide quinoa among bowls. Top with roasted vegetables.
4. **Drizzle Sauce:** Drizzle peanut sauce over the bowls.
5. **Garnish:** Sprinkle with chopped peanuts and fresh cilantro.

GRILLED CHICKEN WITH HERB-MARINATED ARTICHOKE AND OLIVE SALAD

INGREDIENTS:

Servings

Servings: 4

Preparation Time

15 minutes

Cooking Time

20 minutes

- 4 chicken breasts, boneless and skinless
- 2 tablespoons olive oil
- 1 teaspoon dried oregano
- Salt and freshly ground black pepper, to taste
- 1 cup artichoke hearts, quartered (canned or jarred in water)
- 1/2 cup Kalamata olives, pitted and halved
- 1/4 cup red onion, thinly sliced
- 1/4 cup fresh parsley, chopped
- Juice of 1 lemon
- Additional olive oil for dressing
- Lemon wedges for serving

INSTRUCTIONS:

1. **Preheat Grill:** Preheat your grill to medium-high heat.
2. **Prepare Chicken:** Drizzle chicken breasts with olive oil, oregano, salt, and pepper. Ensure they are evenly coated.
3. **Grill Chicken:** Place chicken on the grill and cook for about 6-7 minutes per side, or until fully cooked and internal temperature reaches 165°F (74°C).
4. **Make Salad:** While the chicken is cooking, combine artichoke hearts, olives, red onion, and parsley in a mixing bowl. Squeeze fresh lemon juice over the top, drizzle with a bit more olive oil, and toss to combine. Season with salt and pepper to taste.
5. **Serve:** Once chicken is grilled, serve each breast with a generous portion of the artichoke and olive salad. Garnish with lemon wedges.

SWEET POTATO AND CHICKPEA BUDDHA BOWL

Servings

4

Preparation Time

15 minutes

Cooking Time

30 minutes

INSTRUCTIONS:

1. **Roast Sweet Potatoes and Chickpeas:** Preheat oven to 400°F (200°C). Toss sweet potatoes and chickpeas with olive oil, garlic powder, salt, and pepper. Spread on a baking sheet and roast for 25-30 minutes, stirring halfway through.
2. **Prepare Dressing:** In a small bowl, whisk together tahini, maple syrup, and lemon juice until smooth.
3. **Assemble Bowls:** Divide spinach among bowls. Top with roasted sweet potatoes, chickpeas, and avocado slices.
4. **Serve:** Drizzle tahini dressing over each bowl and serve immediately.

INGREDIENTS:

- 2 large sweet potatoes, peeled and cubed
- 1 can (15 oz) chickpeas, drained, rinsed, and dried
- 1 avocado, sliced
- 4 cups spinach
- 1/4 cup tahini
- 2 tablespoons maple syrup
- 2 tablespoons lemon juice
- 1 teaspoon garlic powder
- Salt and pepper to taste
- Olive oil

CHICKPEA SPINACH SALAD WITH LEMON TAHINI DRESSING

Servings
4

Preparation Time
15 minutes

INGREDIENTS:

- 2 cans (15 oz each) chickpeas, drained and rinsed
- 4 cups fresh spinach, roughly chopped
- 1 cucumber, diced
- 1 red bell pepper, diced
- 1/4 cup red onion, thinly sliced
- 1/4 cup tahini
- Juice of 1 lemon
- 2 tablespoons water
- 1 garlic clove, minced
- Salt and pepper to taste
- 1 tablespoon olive oil

INSTRUCTIONS:

1. **Prepare Salad:** In a large bowl, combine chickpeas, spinach, cucumber, bell pepper, and red onion.
2. **Make Dressing:** In a small bowl, whisk together tahini, lemon juice, water, minced garlic, salt, and pepper until smooth and creamy.
3. **Dress Salad:** Drizzle the tahini dressing over the salad and toss to coat evenly.
4. **Serve:** Drizzle with olive oil before serving. Enjoy this nutrient-rich salad that's perfect for a filling lunch or a light dinner.

VEGAN ROASTED BEET AND WALNUT SALAD

Servings
4

Preparation Time
15 minutes

Cooking Time
45 minutes

INGREDIENTS:

- 4 medium beets, peeled and cubed
- 1 tablespoon olive oil
- Salt and pepper, to taste
- 1 cup walnuts, roughly chopped
- 2 cups arugula
- 1 small red onion, thinly sliced
- 1/4 cup balsamic vinegar
- 1 tablespoon maple syrup
- 1 teaspoon Dijon mustard
- 1/4 cup extra virgin olive oil
- 1/4 cup orange juice
- Fresh mint leaves, for garnish

INSTRUCTIONS:

1. **Roast Beets:** Preheat your oven to 400°F (200°C). Toss cubed beets with 1 tablespoon olive oil, salt, and pepper. Spread on a baking sheet and roast for about 45 minutes, stirring halfway through, until tender and caramelized.
2. **Prepare Dressing:** While the beets are roasting, whisk together balsamic vinegar, maple syrup, Dijon mustard, extra virgin olive oil, and orange juice in a small bowl. Season with salt and pepper to taste.
3. **Assemble Salad:** In a large salad bowl, combine roasted beets, walnuts, arugula, and red onion. Drizzle with the prepared dressing and toss gently to combine.
4. **Serve:** Garnish with fresh mint leaves before serving.

CREAMY VEGAN CAULIFLOWER SOUP

Servings
4

Preparation Time
10 minutes

Cooking Time
20 minutes

INGREDIENTS:

- 1 head cauliflower, chopped
- 1 onion, chopped
- 2 cloves garlic, minced
- 4 cups vegetable broth
- 1 cup coconut milk
- 2 tablespoons olive oil
- Salt and pepper to taste
- Chopped chives for garnish

INSTRUCTIONS:

1. **Cook Vegetables:** In a large pot, heat olive oil over medium heat. Add onion and garlic, sauté until softened. Add cauliflower and cook for a few more minutes.
2. **Simmer:** Add vegetable broth and bring to a boil. Reduce heat and simmer until cauliflower is tender, about 15-20 minutes.
3. **Blend Soup:** Use an immersion blender to puree the soup until smooth.
4. **Add Coconut Milk:** Stir in coconut milk, and heat through.
5. **Season:** Adjust salt and pepper to taste.
6. **Serve:** Garnish with chopped chives and serve hot.

CURRIED CAULIFLOWER SOUP

Servings
4

Preparation Time
10 minutes

Cooking Time
25 minutes

INGREDIENTS:

- 1 head cauliflower, chopped into florets
- 1 onion, chopped
- 2 cloves garlic, minced
- 1 apple, peeled and diced
- 1 tablespoon curry powder
- 4 cups vegetable broth
- 1 can coconut milk
- Salt and pepper to taste
- Olive oil
- Fresh cilantro for garnish

INSTRUCTIONS:

1. **Sauté Onions and Garlic:** In a large pot, heat olive oil over medium heat. Add onion and garlic, sauté until onion is translucent.
2. **Add Curry Powder:** Stir in curry powder and cook for 1 minute until fragrant.
3. **Cook Cauliflower and Apple:** Add cauliflower and apple to the pot, stir to coat with the curry mixture.
4. **Simmer:** Add vegetable broth and bring to a boil. Reduce heat and simmer for 20 minutes, until cauliflower is tender.
5. **Blend Soup:** Use an immersion blender to puree the soup until smooth.
6. **Stir in Coconut Milk:** Add coconut milk and heat through. Adjust seasoning with salt and pepper.
7. **Serve:** Garnish with fresh cilantro and a drizzle of olive oil.

QUINOA AND BLACK BEAN STUFFED PEPPERS

Servings	Preparation Time	Cooking Time
4	20 minutes	30 minutes

INGREDIENTS:

- 4 large bell peppers, halved and seeded
- 1 cup cooked quinoa
- 1 can (15 oz) black beans, drained and rinsed
- 1 cup corn kernels (fresh or frozen)
- 1 small red onion, chopped
- 1/2 cup chopped cilantro
- 1 teaspoon cumin
- 1/2 teaspoon chili powder
- 1 lime, juiced
- 1/2 cup tomato sauce
- Salt and pepper to taste
- 1 tablespoon olive oil

INSTRUCTIONS:

1. **Preheat Oven:** Preheat oven to 375°F (190°C).
2. **Prepare Filling:** In a large bowl, mix together quinoa, black beans, corn, red onion, cilantro, cumin, chili powder, lime juice, and tomato sauce. Season with salt and pepper.
3. **Stuff Peppers:** Brush the outside of the peppers with olive oil and fill each pepper half with the quinoa mixture.
4. **Bake:** Place stuffed peppers in a baking dish, cover with foil, and bake for 30 minutes or until the peppers are tender.
5. **Serve:** Serve warm, topped with avocado slices or a dollop of vegan sour cream.

THAI-INSPIRED VEGAN GREEN CURRY

Servings: 4

Preparation Time

15 minutes

Cooking Time

25 minutes

INGREDIENTS:

- 1 tablespoon coconut oil
- 1 medium onion, finely chopped
- 3 cloves garlic, minced
- 1 tablespoon fresh ginger, minced
- 2 tablespoons Thai green curry paste (ensure it's vegan)
- 1 can (14 oz) coconut milk
- 2 cups vegetable broth
- 1 large carrot, sliced thinly
- 1 red bell pepper, sliced
- 1 cup baby corn (fresh or canned)
- 1 cup tofu, cubed (pressed and drained)
- 2 tablespoons soy sauce or tamari
- 1 tablespoon maple syrup or coconut sugar
- Juice of 1 lime
- Fresh basil or cilantro for garnish
- Cooked jasmine rice or rice noodles for serving

INSTRUCTIONS:

1. **Prepare the Tofu and Aromatics:** Sauté tofu cubes in a pan until golden brown. Set aside. In the same pan, heat coconut oil and cook chopped onion until translucent, then add garlic and ginger until fragrant.
2. **Add Curry Paste:** Stir in green curry paste and cook for 2 minutes to release its flavors.
3. Add coconut milk and vegetable broth, then mix in carrots, bell pepper, and baby corn. Simmer until vegetables are tender.
4. **Incorporate Tofu and Flavorings:** Return tofu to the pan. Stir in soy sauce, maple syrup, and lime juice. Adjust seasoning as needed.
5. **Serve:** Serve the curry over jasmine rice or rice noodles. Garnish with fresh basil or cilantro.

VEGAN MOROCCAN SPICED CHICKPEA SOUP

INGREDIENTS:

Servings

Servings: 4

Preparation Time

10 minutes

Cooking Time

25 minutes

- 2 tablespoons olive oil
- 1 large onion, diced
- 2 garlic cloves, minced
- 1 teaspoon ground cumin
- 1 teaspoon ground coriander
- 1/2 teaspoon ground cinnamon
- 1/2 teaspoon ground turmeric
- 1/4 teaspoon cayenne pepper
- 2 cups vegetable broth
- 1 can (15 oz) diced tomatoes, undrained
- 1 can (15 oz) chickpeas, drained and rinsed
- 1 carrot, peeled and diced
- 1 zucchini, diced
- Salt and pepper to taste
- Fresh cilantro, chopped for garnish
- Lemon wedges, for serving

INSTRUCTIONS:

1. **Heat Oil:** In a large pot, heat olive oil over medium heat. Add onion and garlic, sauté until onion is translucent.
2. **Add Spices:** Stir in cumin, coriander, cinnamon, turmeric, and cayenne. Cook for about 1 minute until fragrant.
3. **Simmer Soup:** Add vegetable broth, diced tomatoes with their juice, chickpeas, carrot, and zucchini. Bring to a boil, then reduce heat and simmer for 20 minutes, or until vegetables are tender.
4. **Season:** Taste and adjust seasoning with salt and pepper.
5. **Garnish and Serve:** Ladle the soup into bowls, garnish with chopped cilantro, and serve with a wedge of lemon on the side.

VEGAN LENTIL SOUP

Servings

6

Preparation Time

10 minutes

Cooking Time

45 minutes

INGREDIENTS:

- 1 cup dried lentils, rinsed
- 1 large carrot, diced
- 2 celery stalks, diced
- 1 onion, diced
- 3 cloves garlic, minced
- 1 can (14 oz) diced tomatoes
- 6 cups vegetable broth
- 2 teaspoons herbs de Provence
- Salt and pepper to taste
- Olive oil

INSTRUCTIONS:

1. **Sauté Vegetables:** In a large pot, heat olive oil over medium heat. Add carrots, celery, onion, and garlic. Cook until vegetables are softened, about 5 minutes.
2. **Simmer Soup:** Add lentils, diced tomatoes, vegetable broth, and herbs de Provence. Bring to a boil, then reduce heat and simmer for 35-40 minutes, or until lentils are tender.
3. **Season:** Adjust seasoning with salt and pepper.
4. **Serve:** Serve hot, garnished with fresh parsley or a swirl of olive oil.

VEGAN MANGO COCONUT SMOOTHIE

Servings
2

Preparation Time
5 minutes

INGREDIENTS:

- 1 ripe mango, peeled and cubed
- 1 banana
- 1 cup coconut milk
- 1/2 teaspoon vanilla extract
- Ice cubes

INSTRUCTIONS:

1. **Blend Ingredients:** In a blender, combine mango, banana, coconut milk, vanilla extract, and ice cubes.
2. **Process:** Blend on high until smooth and creamy.
3. **Serve:** Pour into glasses and enjoy immediately for a tropical, energy-boosting drink.

VEGAN TOFU SCRAMBLE WITH SPINACH

Servings
2

Preparation Time
10 minutes

Cooking Time
10 minutes

INGREDIENTS:

- 1 block firm tofu, drained and crumbled
- 2 cups fresh spinach
- 1/2 red bell pepper, diced
- 1 small onion, diced
- 1 teaspoon turmeric
- 1/2 teaspoon garlic powder
- 1/2 teaspoon black salt (kala namak) for eggy flavor
- 2 tablespoons nutritional yeast
- 1 tablespoon olive oil
- Fresh black pepper to taste
- Fresh parsley or cilantro, chopped for garnish

INSTRUCTIONS:

1. **Sauté Vegetables:** In a skillet, heat olive oil over medium heat. Add onion and bell pepper, sauté until softened, about 5 minutes.
2. **Add Tofu and Seasonings:** Add crumbled tofu, turmeric, garlic powder, and black salt. Cook, stirring frequently, for about 5 minutes.
3. **Add Spinach:** Stir in spinach and cook until just wilted.
4. **Season with Nutritional Yeast:** Sprinkle nutritional yeast over the scramble and stir to combine. Season with black pepper.
5. **Garnish and Serve:** Garnish with fresh parsley or cilantro. Serve hot with toasted whole-grain bread or as part of a larger breakfast spread.

VEGAN ROASTED BRUSSELS SPROUTS AND CARROT MEDLEY

Servings
4

Preparation Time
10 minutes

Cooking Time
25 minutes

INSTRUCTIONS:

1. **Preheat Oven:** Set oven to 400°F (200°C).
2. **Prepare Vegetables:** Toss Brussels sprouts and carrots with olive oil, smoked paprika, salt, and pepper. Spread on a baking sheet.
3. **Roast:** Bake for 20-25 minutes, stirring halfway through, until vegetables are tender and caramelized.
4. **Finish with Balsamic:** Drizzle balsamic vinegar over roasted vegetables in the last 5 minutes of cooking.
5. **Add Nuts:** Sprinkle walnuts over the vegetables right after taking them out of the oven.
6. **Garnish and Serve:** Top with fresh parsley before serving alongside your favorite grain or protein source for a complete meal.

INGREDIENTS:

- 3 cups Brussels sprouts, halved
- 2 large carrots, sliced diagonally
- 1 tablespoon olive oil
- 1 teaspoon smoked paprika
- Salt and pepper to taste
- 2 tablespoons balsamic vinegar
- 1/4 cup chopped walnuts
- Fresh parsley, chopped for garnish

SPICY BLACK BEAN AND QUINOA BURGERS

Servings
4

Preparation Time
20 minutes

Cooking Time
10 minutes

INSTRUCTIONS:

1. **Mash Beans:** In a bowl, mash black beans until mostly smooth.
2. **Mix Ingredients:** Add cooked quinoa, breadcrumbs, red onion, garlic, cumin, smoked paprika, chili powder, salt, and pepper to the mashed beans. Mix until well combined.
3. **Form Patties:** Divide the mixture into four equal parts and form into burger patties.
4. **Cook Burgers:** In a skillet, heat olive oil over medium heat. Cook the burgers for about 5 minutes on each side until they are firm and have a crispy exterior.
5. **Serve:** Serve on gluten-free burger buns with your favorite toppings like avocado, lettuce, tomato, and vegan mayo.

INGREDIENTS:

- 1 cup cooked quinoa
- 1 can black beans, drained and rinsed
- 1/2 cup breadcrumbs (gluten-free if needed)
- 1/4 cup finely chopped red onion
- 1 clove garlic, minced
- 1 teaspoon cumin
- 1/2 teaspoon smoked paprika
- 1/4 teaspoon chili powder
- Salt and pepper to taste
- 2 tablespoons olive oil

CHICKPEA AVOCADO SALAD

Servings

2

Preparation Time

10 minutes

INGREDIENTS:

- 1 can (15 oz) chickpeas, drained and rinsed
- 1 ripe avocado, diced
- 1/4 cup chopped red onion
- 1/4 cup chopped cilantro
- Juice of 1 lime
- Salt and pepper to taste
- 1 tablespoon olive oil

INSTRUCTIONS:

1. **Combine Salad Ingredients:** In a bowl, combine chickpeas, diced avocado, red onion, and cilantro.
2. **Dress Salad:** Add lime juice, olive oil, salt, and pepper. Gently toss to combine without breaking the avocado pieces.
3. **Serve:** This salad can be enjoyed on its own or as a filling for wraps. It's refreshing, filling, and packed with proteins and healthy fats.

VEGAN COCONUT CURRY SOUP

Servings

4

Preparation Time

10 minutes

Cooking Time

20 minutes

INGREDIENTS:

- 1 tablespoon coconut oil
- 1 onion, diced
- 2 cloves garlic, minced
- 1 tablespoon grated ginger
- 1 tablespoon curry powder
- 1 can (14 oz) coconut milk
- 4 cups vegetable broth
- 1 sweet potato, peeled and diced
- 1 red bell pepper, diced
- 1 cup chopped kale
- Salt and pepper to taste
- Fresh cilantro for garnish

INSTRUCTIONS:

1. **Sauté Aromatics:** In a large pot, heat coconut oil over medium heat. Add onion, garlic, and ginger, and sauté until onion is translucent.
2. **Add Curry:** Stir in curry powder and cook for 1 minute until fragrant.
3. **Simmer Vegetables:** Add coconut milk, vegetable broth, sweet potato, and bell pepper. Bring to a boil, then reduce heat and simmer for 15 minutes, or until sweet potatoes are tender.
4. **Add Kale:** Stir in kale and cook until wilted, about 5 minutes.
5. **Season and Serve:** Season with salt and pepper. Garnish with fresh cilantro before serving.

CHAPTER 10: SNACKS AND BEVERAGES FOR OPTIMAL ENERGY: DELICIOUS RECIPES

Step into a vibrant world of flavors and freshness where every sip and bite is designed to elevate your energy and enrich your health. In Chapter 10, we explore a palette of snacks and beverages that do more than just tide you over to the next meal—they infuse your day with bursts of vitality and moments of pure culinary delight.

Imagine starting your morning or refreshing your afternoon with a Matcha Green Tea Smoothie, its brilliant green hue as invigorating to look at as it is revitalizing to drink. Each smooth blend of matcha powder not only awakens the senses but also floods your body with antioxidants.

Crunch into Spicy Roasted Chickpeas, where each kernel pops with bold spices that tickle your palate while packing a protein punch that powers you through any slump. Or, indulge in Almond and Date Energy Balls, where the natural sweetness of dates meets the nutty crunch of almonds in a dance of flavors that are as satisfying as they are sustaining.

Refresh with a glass of Cucumber Lemon Water or Ginger Lemon Honey Tea, each gulp a gulp of detoxification, hydration, and pure, clean taste that cleanses your palate and clears your mind.

As the sun sets, unwind with a Golden Milk Turmeric Tea, a comforting concoction that combines the soothing warmth of milk with the healing properties of turmeric, cradling you in comfort and preparing you for a restful night.

From the savory richness of Avocado Toast with Pumpkin Seeds to the sweet, tangy zing of a Coconut Water and Pineapple Smoothie, this chapter offers a treasure trove of tastes that are not only delightful but are also crafted to support a healthy, energetic lifestyle. Dive into these pages and discover how each snack and drink is a stepping stone to sustained energy and wellness, transforming your daily eating habits into a joyful, healthful ritual.

MATCHA GREEN TEA SMOOTHIE

Servings

1

Preparation Time

5 minutes

INSTRUCTIONS:

1. **Blend Ingredients:** In a blender, combine matcha powder, banana, spinach, almond milk, and honey if using. Add a handful of ice cubes.
2. **Process:** Blend on high until smooth and creamy.
3. **Serve:** Pour into a glass and enjoy immediately. This smoothie is perfect for a morning or afternoon energy boost, providing antioxidants and nutrients.

INGREDIENTS:

- 1 teaspoon matcha green tea powder
- 1 banana
- 1/2 cup spinach leaves
- 1 cup unsweetened almond milk
- 1 tablespoon honey (optional)
- Ice cubes

SPICY ROASTED CHICKPEAS

Servings

5

Preparation Time

5 minutes

Cooking Time

30 minutes

INSTRUCTIONS:

1. **Preheat Oven:** Preheat oven to 400°F (200°C).
2. **Season Chickpeas:** Toss chickpeas with olive oil, chili powder, cumin, and salt.
3. **Roast:** Spread chickpeas on a baking sheet in a single layer. Roast for 30 minutes, shaking the pan occasionally, until crispy and golden.
4. **Serve:** Let cool and serve as a crunchy, spicy snack. These are great for a portable energy boost.

INGREDIENTS:

- 1 can (15 oz) chickpeas, drained, rinsed, and dried
- 1 tablespoon olive oil
- 1/2 teaspoon chili powder
- 1/2 teaspoon cumin
- Salt to taste

ALMOND AND DATE ENERGY BALLS

Servings

10

Preparation Time

15 minutes

INGREDIENTS:

- 1 cup pitted dates
- 1/2 cup raw almonds
- 1/2 cup shredded coconut
- 1 tablespoon chia seeds
- 1 tablespoon flaxseeds
- 1 teaspoon vanilla extract

INSTRUCTIONS:

1. **Process Ingredients:** In a food processor, combine dates, almonds, shredded coconut, chia seeds, flaxseeds, and vanilla extract. Process until the mixture forms a sticky dough.
2. **Form Balls:** Roll the mixture into small balls, about 1 inch in diameter.
3. **Chill:** Refrigerate the balls for at least 1 hour to set.
4. **Serve:** Enjoy these as a nutritious snack that delivers a sustainable energy boost throughout the day.

AVOCADO TOAST WITH PUMPKIN SEEDS

Servings

2

Preparation Time

5 minutes

INGREDIENTS:

- 2 slices whole grain bread
- 1 ripe avocado
- Lemon juice
- Salt and pepper to taste
- 2 tablespoons pumpkin seeds, toasted

INSTRUCTIONS:

1. **Toast Bread:** Toast the bread slices to your desired level of crispiness.
2. **Prepare Avocado:** In a bowl, mash the avocado with a fork. Season with lemon juice, salt, and pepper.
3. **Assemble:** Spread the mashed avocado evenly on each slice of toasted bread. Sprinkle toasted pumpkin seeds on top.
4. **Serve:** Enjoy immediately for a satisfying snack that combines healthy fats, fiber, and protein for balanced energy levels.

GREEK YOGURT PARFAIT WITH MIXED BERRIES AND GRANOLA

Servings

1

Preparation Time

5 minutes

INGREDIENTS:

- 1 cup Greek yogurt
- 1/2 cup mixed berries (strawberries, blueberries, raspberries)
- 1/4 cup granola
- 1 tablespoon honey or maple syrup (optional)
- A sprinkle of cinnamon (optional)

INSTRUCTIONS:

1. **Layer Parfait:** In a glass or bowl, start with a layer of Greek yogurt.
2. **Add Berries:** Add a layer of mixed berries.
3. **Top with Granola:** Sprinkle granola over the berries.
4. **Drizzle Honey:** If using, drizzle honey or maple syrup over the top.
5. **Repeat Layers:** Repeat the layering if desired or if the size of your container allows.
6. **Serve:** Finish with a sprinkle of cinnamon for extra flavor. Enjoy this energy-boosting parfait as a healthy breakfast or an afternoon snack.

CUCUMBER LEMON WATER

Servings

2

Preparation Time

5 minutes

INGREDIENTS:

- 1/2 cucumber, thinly sliced
- 1 lemon, thinly sliced
- 4 cups water
- Ice cubes
- Fresh mint leaves (optional)

INSTRUCTIONS:

1. **Prepare Water:** In a large pitcher, combine sliced cucumber, lemon, and fresh mint if using.
2. **Add Water and Ice:** Fill the pitcher with water and add a handful of ice cubes.
3. **Chill:** Let the water chill in the refrigerator for at least 30 minutes to allow the flavors to infuse.
4. **Serve:** Pour into glasses and enjoy a refreshing, hydrating drink that helps maintain optimal hydration and energy levels.

SPINACH AND FETA MINI QUICHES

Servings

12

Preparation Time
15 minutes

Cooking Time
25 minutes

INGREDIENTS:

- 4 eggs
- 1 cup chopped spinach
- 1/2 cup crumbled feta cheese
- 1/4 cup diced onions
- 1/4 cup milk
- Salt and pepper to taste
- Cooking spray or oil for greasing

INSTRUCTIONS:

1. **Preheat Oven:** Preheat your oven to 350°F (175°C). Grease a mini muffin tin with cooking spray or oil.
2. **Combine Ingredients:** In a bowl, whisk together eggs, milk, salt, and pepper. Stir in chopped spinach, crumbled feta, and diced onions.
3. **Fill Muffin Tin:** Spoon the mixture into the greased mini muffin tin, filling each cup about 3/4 full.
4. **Bake:** Bake in the preheated oven for 25 minutes or until the eggs are set and the tops are slightly golden.
5. **Serve:** Let cool for a few minutes before removing from the tin. Enjoy warm or at room temperature for a protein-rich, energizing snack.

CARROT AND GINGER JUICE

Servings

2

Preparation Time
10 minutes

INGREDIENTS:

- 4 large carrots, peeled and chopped
- 1-inch piece of fresh ginger, peeled
- 1 apple, cored and sliced
- 1/2 lemon, juiced

INSTRUCTIONS:

1. **Juice Ingredients:** Using a juicer, process the carrots, ginger, and apple.
2. **Add Lemon Juice:** Stir in the fresh lemon juice to the mixed juice.
3. **Serve:** Pour into glasses and serve immediately for a refreshing and invigorating boost of vitamins and antioxidants.

SWEET POTATO CHIPS WITH AVOCADO DIP

Servings

4

Preparation Time

10 minutes

Cooking Time

20 minutes

INGREDIENTS:

- 2 large sweet potatoes, thinly sliced
- 2 tablespoons olive oil
- Salt and smoked paprika to taste
- 1 ripe avocado
- Juice of 1 lime
- 1 clove garlic, minced
- A pinch of cayenne pepper (optional)

INSTRUCTIONS:

1. **Preheat Oven:** Preheat your oven to 375°F (190°C). Line a baking sheet with parchment paper.
2. **Prepare Sweet Potatoes:** Toss the sliced sweet potatoes with olive oil, salt, and smoked paprika. Spread in a single layer on the prepared baking sheet.
3. **Bake Chips:** Bake for 20 minutes, turning halfway through, until crisp and golden.
4. **Make Avocado Dip:** While chips are baking, mash the avocado in a bowl. Mix in lime juice, minced garlic, and cayenne pepper if using.
5. **Serve:** Serve the baked sweet potato chips with the creamy avocado dip for a tasty and energizing snack.

PROTEIN-PACKED TRAIL MIX

Servings

Multiple

Preparation Time

5 minutes

INGREDIENTS:

- 1 cup raw almonds
- 1 cup raw cashews
- 1/2 cup pumpkin seeds
- 1/2 cup sunflower seeds
- 1/2 cup dried cranberries
- 1/2 cup dark chocolate chips

INSTRUCTIONS:

1. **Mix Ingredients:** In a large bowl, combine almonds, cashews, pumpkin seeds, sunflower seeds, dried cranberries, and dark chocolate chips.
2. **Toss:** Toss the mixture well to evenly distribute all components.
3. **Store:** Transfer the trail mix to an airtight container for easy storage and portability.
4. **Enjoy:** This trail mix is perfect for a quick snack, providing a good balance of protein, healthy fats, and a touch of sweetness for an energy boost.

GOLDEN MILK TURMERIC TEA

Servings

2

Preparation Time

5 minutes

Cooking Time

10 minutes

INGREDIENTS:

- 2 cups almond milk
- 1 teaspoon turmeric powder
- 1/2 teaspoon cinnamon
- 1/4 teaspoon ginger powder
- 1 pinch black pepper (to enhance turmeric absorption)
- Honey or maple syrup to taste

INSTRUCTIONS:

1. **Heat Ingredients:** In a small pot, combine almond milk, turmeric, cinnamon, ginger, and black pepper. Heat gently over medium heat, but do not allow to boil.
2. **Sweeten:** Add honey or maple syrup to taste, stirring well to combine.
3. **Serve:** Pour the golden milk into mugs. This warm, soothing drink is perfect for relaxing in the evening, promoting inflammation reduction and providing a calm energy release.

WALNUT AND DATE ENERGY BITES

Servings

15

Preparation Time

15 minutes

INGREDIENTS:

- 1 cup dates, pitted
- 1/2 cup walnuts
- 1/2 cup almonds
- 2 tablespoons cocoa powder
- 1 tablespoon chia seeds
- 1 teaspoon vanilla extract
- Desiccated coconut for coating (optional)

INSTRUCTIONS:

1. **Process Ingredients:** In a food processor, combine dates, walnuts, almonds, cocoa powder, chia seeds, and vanilla extract. Process until the mixture forms a sticky dough.
2. **Form Bites:** Roll the mixture into small balls, about the size of a walnut.
3. **Coat in Coconut:** If using, roll each ball in desiccated coconut to coat.
4. **Chill:** Refrigerate the bites for at least 1 hour to firm up.
5. **Serve:** Enjoy these walnut and date energy bites as a quick, portable snack perfect for a pre-workout boost or midday pick-me-up.

AVOCADO LIME SMOOTHIE

Servings
1

Preparation Time
5 minutes

INGREDIENTS:

- 1 ripe avocado, peeled and pitted
- Juice of 1 lime
- 1/2 banana
- 1 cup spinach
- 1 cup coconut water
- 1 tablespoon honey (optional)
- Ice cubes

INSTRUCTIONS:

1. **Blend Ingredients:** In a blender, combine avocado, lime juice, banana, spinach, coconut water, honey (if using), and ice cubes.
2. **Process:** Blend on high until smooth and creamy.
3. **Serve:** Pour into a glass and enjoy a creamy, nutrient-rich smoothie that provides a sustained energy boost with healthy fats and electrolytes.

KALE AND ALMOND PESTO DIP

Servings
4

Preparation Time
10 minutes

INGREDIENTS:

- 2 cups fresh kale, stems removed
- 1/2 cup almonds, toasted
- 1/2 cup grated Parmesan cheese
- 2 cloves garlic
- Juice of 1 lemon
- 1/2 cup olive oil
- Salt and pepper to taste

INSTRUCTIONS:

1. **Blend Ingredients:** In a food processor, combine kale, almonds, Parmesan cheese, garlic, and lemon juice. Pulse to combine.
2. **Add Olive Oil:** While the processor is running, slowly add olive oil until the mixture reaches a smooth consistency.
3. **Season:** Add salt and pepper to taste.
4. **Serve:** Enjoy this pesto dip with whole-grain crackers or sliced vegetables for a refreshing and energizing snack.

COCONUT WATER AND PINEAPPLE SMOOTHIE

Servings

2

Preparation Time

5 minutes

INSTRUCTIONS:

1. **Blend Ingredients:** In a blender, combine coconut water, pineapple, banana, and chia seeds.
2. **Process:** Blend on high until smooth.
3. **Serve:** Pour into glasses and serve immediately for a hydrating and energizing drink that's perfect for post-workout recovery.

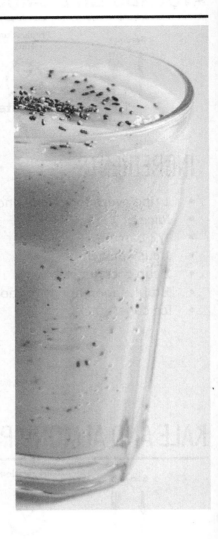

INGREDIENTS:

- 1 cup coconut water
- 1 cup frozen pineapple chunks
- 1/2 banana
- 1 tablespoon chia seeds

CUCUMBER MINT WATER

Servings

4

Preparation Time

5 minutes

INSTRUCTIONS:

1. **Prepare Water:** In a large pitcher, add sliced cucumber and fresh mint leaves.
2. **Add Water:** Fill the pitcher with water and stir gently to combine.
3. **Chill:** Refrigerate for at least 1 hour to allow the flavors to infuse.
4. **Serve:** Pour over ice for a refreshing and hydrating drink that helps to maintain optimal hydration and energy levels throughout the day.

INGREDIENTS:

- 1 large cucumber, thinly sliced
- 10 fresh mint leaves
- 1 gallon of water
- Ice cubes

SWEET AND SPICY NUTS

Servings
Multiple

Preparation Time
5 minutes

Cooking Time
10 minutes

INGREDIENTS:

- 2 cups mixed nuts (e.g., almonds, pecans, walnuts)
- 1 tablespoon maple syrup
- 1 tablespoon olive oil
- 1/2 teaspoon cayenne pepper
- 1/2 teaspoon cinnamon
- Salt to taste

INSTRUCTIONS:

1. **Preheat Oven:** Preheat your oven to 350°F (175°C).
2. **Season Nuts:** In a bowl, combine nuts with maple syrup, olive oil, cayenne pepper, cinnamon, and salt.
3. **Bake:** Spread the nuts on a baking sheet lined with parchment paper. Bake for 10 minutes, stirring halfway through to ensure even cooking.
4. **Cool and Serve:** Allow the nuts to cool before serving. These sweet and spicy nuts are ideal for a quick energy boost.

SPICED WALNUTS

Servings
Multiple

Preparation Time
5 minutes

Cooking Time
10 minutes

INGREDIENTS:

- 2 cups walnuts
- 1 tablespoon maple syrup
- 1 teaspoon cinnamon
- 1/2 teaspoon nutmeg
- A pinch of salt

INSTRUCTIONS:

1. **Preheat Oven:** Preheat your oven to 350°F (175°C).
2. **Season Walnuts:** In a bowl, toss walnuts with maple syrup, cinnamon, nutmeg, and salt.
3. **Bake:** Spread the walnuts on a baking sheet lined with parchment paper. Bake for 10 minutes or until toasted and fragrant.
4. **Cool and Serve:** Let the walnuts cool completely before serving. This snack is great for a quick energy boost, thanks to the healthy fats and protein in walnuts.

GINGER LEMON HONEY TEA

Servings

2

Preparation Time

5 minutes

Cooking Time

10 minutes

INGREDIENTS:

- 2 cups water
- 1-inch piece of fresh ginger, thinly sliced
- Juice of 1 lemon
- 2 tablespoons honey

INSTRUCTIONS:

1. **Simmer Ginger:** In a small pot, bring water and ginger slices to a boil. Reduce heat and simmer for 10 minutes.
2. **Add Lemon and Honey:** Remove from heat. Stir in lemon juice and honey until well combined.
3. **Serve:** Strain the tea into cups. This warming drink is perfect for boosting immunity and energy, especially during colder months.

SPICED TURKEY LETTUCE WRAPS

Servings

4

Preparation Time

10 minutes

Cooking Time

10 minutes

INGREDIENTS:

- 1 lb ground turkey
- 1 tablespoon olive oil
- 1 teaspoon garlic powder
- 1 teaspoon ground cumin
- 1/2 teaspoon chili powder
- Salt and pepper to taste
- 1 head iceberg lettuce, leaves separated to form cups
- 1/2 cup diced tomatoes
- 1/4 cup shredded carrots
- 1 avocado, diced
- Fresh cilantro, for garnish
- Lime wedges, for serving

INSTRUCTIONS:

1. **Cook Turkey:** In a skillet, heat olive oil over medium heat. Add ground turkey, breaking it up with a spatula. Cook until browned, about 5-7 minutes.
2. **Season:** Add garlic powder, cumin, chili powder, salt, and pepper to the turkey. Stir well to combine and cook for another 2-3 minutes until fragrant.
3. **Prepare Lettuce Cups:** Lay out lettuce leaves on a serving platter. Spoon the cooked turkey mixture into each lettuce cup.
4. **Add Toppings:** Top each wrap with diced tomatoes, shredded carrots, and diced avocado.
5. **Garnish and Serve:** Garnish with fresh cilantro and serve with lime wedges on the side.

CONCLUSION: A JOURNEY TO VIBRANT HEALTH THROUGH GOOD ENERGY CUISINE

As you close this book, you carry with you more than just a collection of recipes; you hold a new perspective on eating that elevates your daily energy and transforms your approach to health. Each chapter has been carefully curated not only to introduce you to a range of delicious, nutritious meals but to inspire a lifelong journey of vibrant health powered by what you eat.

From the energizing breakfasts that kickstart your metabolic engine to the restorative dinners that heal and recharge your body after a long day, you have discovered how each meal can be an opportunity to nourish not only your body but also your soul. The plant-based and vegan dishes underscore a commitment to ethical, sustainable eating, while the snacks and beverages section ensures that every craving and need for a quick energy boost is met with a healthy, tasty option.

Embrace these recipes as your toolkit for health. Let the spices, herbs, fruits, and vegetables bring color to your plate and vitality to your body. Remember that each ingredient was chosen to enhance your energy, support your body's natural rhythms, and provide the nutrition you need to thrive.

Now, with this book in your kitchen, you're equipped not just to follow recipes, but to innovate your own. You're ready to make each meal an act of self-care, an affirmation of your desire for health, and a celebration of the abundant possibilities that good, wholesome food brings to your life.

Go forth and cook with confidence, creativity, and joy. May your meals be as fulfilling as they are delicious, and may your journey through the pages of this book inspire an ever-deepening appreciation for the power of nourishing food. Welcome to the vibrant life you deserve, powered by good energy cuisine.

Made in the USA
Las Vegas, NV
30 November 2024